engage

In **engage** this issue we're fu~~~ ~~~
Isn't the Bible irrelevant now? How do you expl~~~~ ~~~
gospel? What on earth is a Thessalonian? How do I
understand the Bible? Aren't snowboarders too cool to
be Christians? Read on and discover the answers with us.

✱ DAILY READINGS Each day's
page throws you into the Bible, to
get you handling, questioning and
exploring God's message to you —
encouraging you to act on it and talk
to God more in prayer.

THIS ISSUE: Search for a king in
1 Samuel; grow as a Christian with
2 Thessalonians; expand your view
of God with **Isaiah;** and travel the
globe with Paul in **Acts.**

✱ TAKE IT FURTHER If you're
hungry for more at the end of an
engage page, turn to the **Take it
further** section to dig deeper.

✱ ESSENTIAL Articles on the
basics we really need to know about
God, the Bible and Christianity. This
issue, we ask the question: **What is
the gospel?**

✱ TRICKY tackles those mind-
bendingly tricky questions that
confuse us all, as well as stuff our
friends bombard us with. This time:
Isn't the Bible irrelevant?

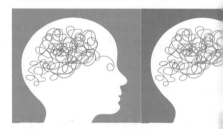

✱ REAL LIVES True stories,
revealing God at work in people's
lives. This time — **Olympic
snowboard champion Kelly Clark.**

✱ STUFF Articles on stuff relevant
to the lives of young Christians.
This issue: **What music should we
listen to?**

✱ TOOLBOX is full of tools
to help you understand the Bible.
This issue we concentrate on **how
to interpret the Bible.**

All of us who work on **engage** are
passionate to see the Bible at
work in people's lives. Do you
want God's word to have an
impact on your life? Then open
your Bible, and start on the first
engage study right now...

1

HOW TO USE engage

1 Set a time you can read the Bible every day

2 Find a place where you can be quiet and think

3 Grab your Bible, pen and a notebook

4 Ask God to help you understand what you read

5 Read the day's verses with **engage**, taking time to think about it

6 Pray about what you've read

BIBLE STUFF We use the NIV Bible version, so you might find it's the best one to use with engage. If the notes say **"1 Samuel 2 v 5–13"**, look up 1 Samuel in the contents page at the front of your Bible. It'll tell you which page the book starts on. Find chapter 2 of 1 Samuel, and then verse 5 of chapter 2 (the verse numbers are the tiny ones). Then start reading. Simple.

In this issue...

ENGAGE IS BROUGHT TO YOU BY

Wordsmiths: Martin Cole   Carl Laferton   Cassie Martin   Helen Thorne
Designer & dreamer: Steve Devane
Proof-reader: Anne Woodcock
Editor: Martin Cole (martin@thegoodbook.co.uk)

1 Samuel

The search for a king

Get ready for an action-packed read. The book of 1 Samuel has a miracle birth, evil priests, ark theft, vicious battles and the search for a great king.

The story continues where Judges left off. God's people, the Israelites, were in Canaan — the land God had promised them. But things were not going well. Despite a series of judges who'd rescued them from God's punishment, they still refused to obey Him. In 1 Samuel, incredibly, God still cared for His unfaithful people. He would still keep His promises and use them in His perfect plans.

In this book we see God appoint Samuel as the last of the judges, then pick Saul as Israel's first king, then David to replace him. You see, a king was now the thing. A big change was underway.

1 Samuel will sharpen our thinking about God: what He's like; what He's doing; what He wants; how He acts.

And it will remind us to look ahead — into the New Testament — for the perfect King chosen by God, who would fully achieve God's plans.

So prepare for a search for a great king with many incidents along the way. 1 Samuel poses the big question: who will be king? Who would lead the Israelites in battle as their king? And more importantly for us, who will be the king of our lives?

Let's start the search...

Family fortunes

1 Samuel opens with the spotlight on a strange little family — one husband, two wives and a bitter rivalry. It can only end in tears.

Read 1 Samuel 1 v 1–8

ENGAGE YOUR BRAIN

▷ What do we learn about this unhappy family?

v2: *Elkanah has 2 wives*

v3: *They all visit Shiloh*

v5: *Elkanah loves Hannah*

v6–7: *Peninnah teases Hannah*

What a miserable way to begin a book! Poor childless Hannah being taunted to tears. And we're even told that *God* had closed her womb (v6). It all seems so unfair. But it was part of God's perfect plan for His people.

Read verses 9–20

▷ What did Hannah do at her lowest point? (v10–11)

prayed

▷ What did Eli the priest think was happening? (v13–14)

Hannah was Drunk

▷ How did he encourage Hannah? (v17–18)

Asked God to help Hannah

▷ What did God do for Hannah? (v19–20)

Give her a child

▷ How did she respond? (v20)

Thank God.

Before: Hannah was miserable and childless, so she took it all to God in prayer. And even promised to give her son over to God.

After: Just talking to God seemed to lift Hannah's spirits (v18). Amazingly, the Lord gave her a little boy. God won't always answer our prayers in the way we want or expect, but we can trust He'll always do what's best for us.

PRAY ABOUT IT

When you pray, pour out your heart to God. Leave your worries with Him. Why not start right now, by talking honestly to God about how you're feeling?

THE BOTTOM LINE

Pour out your heart to God.

→ **TAKE IT FURTHER**

Try page 108 for a little bit more.

4

2 | Bye bye baby

Hannah tearfully asked God for a son, promising to give him over to God, to serve Him in the temple. Miraculously, God gave her a baby boy but would Hannah keep her word?

👁 Read 1 Samuel 1 v 21–28

ENGAGE YOUR BRAIN

▷ *Why didn't Hannah join in with the yearly sacrifice? (v22)*

Because Samuel was not ready

▷ *How did Hannah keep her promise to God? (v24–25)*

Gave Samuel to the temple

▷ *Why? (v27–28)*

Because he was Gods gift so she was giving him back to God

In those days a baby was weaned (stopped being fed its mother's milk) at about 3 years old. It must have been heart-wrenching for Hannah to leave 3-year-old Samuel at the temple. Would she go back to her miserable, tearful ways?

👁 Read 2 Samuel 2 v 1–11

▷ *What did Hannah praise God for? (v1–2)*

Her happiness

▷ *How do v4–8 describe God?*

king of life & death

▷ *What will He do for His people? (v9)*

Protect them

▷ *What about His enemies? (v10)*

Destroy them

Rather than being tearful at seeing her son go, she praised God for miraculously giving her a son and making her so happy. She knew that God is in control of everything (v4–8). He will protect His people ("saints", v9) but punish those who reject Him.

Hannah also glimpsed the future — a time when God's people would be ruled by a king. With Samuel, though, God was miraculously raising up a judge to rescue and lead His people. That's all to come later in 1 Samuel.

PRAY ABOUT IT

Use Hannah's prayer as a guide and:
1. Thank God for specific things He has done for you.
2. Praise Him for what He's like.
3. Praise God for being a fair Judge and for protecting His people.

→ TAKE IT FURTHER

Bye bye! Call in on page 108.

3 | Stealing from God

God had miraculously brought Samuel into the world. Little Sam was now serving God, helping Eli the priest in Shiloh. But the priest's other servants weren't doing such a good job.

👁 Read 1 Samuel 2 v 12–17

ENGAGE YOUR BRAIN
- *What should have been happening? (v13–14)*
- *But what did Eli's sons do even before the meat was offered to God? (v15–16)*
- *What did this show? (v12, v17)*

God had given in instructions (in the book of Leviticus) that a part of some sacrifices should be used as food for the priests. But only *after* it had been offered to God — not *during* the sacrifice, and certainly not *before* it.

👁 Read verses 18–21 & 26

- *How was Samuel different from Eli's sons? (v26)*
- *How did God bless Hannah even more? (v20–21)*

👁 Read verses 22–25

- *What else were Eli's sons doing? (v22)*
- *How did they respond when their father warned them? (v25)*

Verse 25 sounds harsh, but God's judgment is always fair. Because of their continuing sin, God decided to put them to death, and so they didn't listen to Eli's warning. If someone continually refuses to obey God, one day the Lord will confirm that decision and they will be deaf to any warnings. We can't assume we can keep rejecting God and then turn to Him on our deathbed. We must turn to God now, before it's too late.

GET ON WITH IT
- *Who do you need to warn about God's punishment?*
- *Whose warnings and advice do you need to listen to more?*

PRAY ABOUT IT
Pray for people you know who refuse to live God's way. Ask for His mercy so their hearts will soften and they'll turn to Him.

→ TAKE IT FURTHER
Fat facts on page 108.

4 | Punishment and promise

We don't know his name, we don't know where he came from, in fact we know nothing about him. But, suddenly, out of nowhere, a "man of God" came to Eli with a message from God.

👁 Read 1 Samuel 2 v 27–34

ENGAGE YOUR BRAIN

▷ *What had God done for Eli's family? (v27–28)*

▷ *How had they treated this privilege? (v29)*

▷ *How would God punish them?*

God had given these guys the fantastic privilege of serving Him in a special way. But they threw it back in His face. Eli tolerated his sons misusing God's sacrifice and dishonouring the Lord. Eli put his sinful sons before God (v29). We shouldn't let anything come between us and God, not even our family.

God punished Eli's whole family. Both his sons would die and none of the family would live a long life. Eli's family had sinned against God and so God rightly punished them. But it wasn't all bad news...

👁 Read verses 35–36

▷ *What did God promise to do?*

God wasn't going to let this disobedient family stop His plans. Eli and his family would be punished by God and He would raise up a faithful priest in their place. The books of 2 Samuel and 1 Kings say that Zadok was such a priest who served God faithfully.

Despite His people's sins, God would always have a faithful priest. The New Testament tells us that Jesus was the perfect priest — His death was the ultimate sacrifice, which brings us back to God.

PRAY ABOUT IT

Never forget how seriously God treats sin. And remember, whatever people do, God's plans can't be stopped! Spend time talking to God about this stuff and whatever's on your mind.

→ TAKE IT FURTHER

Who on earth was Zadok? Page 108.

Wake-up call

In Old Testament times, God spoke to His people through prophets who had visions telling them what God's message was. The Israelites had stopped listening to God so He didn't speak to them often any more.

👁 Read 1 Samuel 3 v 1–10

ENGAGE YOUR BRAIN
▶ *Who was calling Samuel?*
▶ *Why was this particularly surprising? (v1)*
▶ *What did Eli tell Sam to say to God?*

God is incredibly patient and kind to His people. The Israelites had been mostly ignoring Him for years and yet He still hadn't given up on them. He was even patient with young Samuel — calling out to him three times, waiting for Sam to work out what was going on.

👁 Read verses 11–18
▶ *What was God's frightening message? (v11–14)*
▶ *Why would Eli be punished? (v13)*
▶ *What did Eli rightly recognise about the bad news? (v18)*

👁 Read verses 19–21
▶ *How did God help Samuel? (v19)*
▶ *How did He use Samuel? (v20-21)*

▶ *How did Samuel learn more about God? (v21)*

These days, God doesn't usually speak to us through prophets, visions or late night shouting. But like Samuel, we have God's word. For us, that's the Bible, and that's how God reveals Himself and His plans to us.

GET ON WITH IT
▶ *Do you look elsewhere for God and His guidance?*
▶ *How can you study God's word more and learn more about His Son Jesus?*

PRAY ABOUT IT
Try this over the next week: every time you read the Bible, talk to God first, asking Him to reveal Himself to you. You could even say: *"Speak, Lord — your servant is listening."*

→ TAKE IT FURTHER
Wake up! And find more on page 108.

6 | God's box

Next up is the story of the ark. No, not the one packed with hippos and lemurs, the other one. This was a very special box which... well, you'll find out.

👁 Read 1 Samuel 4 v 1–3

ENGAGE YOUR BRAIN

▶ What was the shock result of the battle?

▶ What did the Israelite leaders rightly recognise? (v3)

▶ But what mistake did they make? (v3)

The ark was a wooden box which contained the Ten Commandments. It represented God's presence with them and reminded them of His great promises to them. But they treated it as a box of tricks that would give them victory in battle.

👁 Read verses 4–11

▶ What effect did the ark have on the Israelites? (v5)

▶ And on the Philistines (v7–8)

▶ But what happened? (v10)

▶ What else? (v11)

A disastrous, death-filled defeat for the Israelites. They had trusted in the ark to save them, rather than God. They used the ark like a lucky charm, but God wanted His people to turn to Him, heart and soul, and ask for His help. Instead, they ignored God and lost the symbol of His presence.

THINK IT THROUGH

Church, crucifixes, communion, baptism, saying the right things. People think these are important but none of them makes us Christians. Only turning to Jesus for forgiveness does that. Only He can change our lives around.

PRAY ABOUT IT

Ask God to help you not to rely on the wrong things, but to trust in Him and turn to Him for help throughout your life.

→ TAKE IT FURTHER

More ark-eology on page 109.

7 | Goodbye God

Three disastrous things have happened: many Israelites have been killed in battle; Eli's sons have died; and worst of all, the ark of the covenant has been stolen. But Eli hasn't heard the news yet.

Read 1 Samuel 4 v 12–18

ENGAGE YOUR BRAIN

▶ *How did the people of Shiloh react to the news? (v13)*

▶ *Which piece of news was more than Eli could stand? (v18)*

The ark was much more than an old box. It was a sign that God was with His people. So when the ark was stolen, Eli knew God had left His people. It was more than Eli could bear — the shock killed him.

Read verses 19–22

▶ *Who else took the news badly?*

▶ *What did the boy's name mean?*

▶ *Why was he called that?*

This was a tragic day for Israel. Many of their men had been killed by the Philistines. As horrific as that was, something far worse happened. The ark of the covenant had left Israel.

God had left His people because they had turned away from Him.

But this wasn't the end of the story. God hadn't left His people for good. In fact, He's already raised up young Samuel as the prophet to lead the Israelites back to living God's way.

THINK IT THROUGH

▶ *Do you ever feel that God has left you?*

▶ *What do you think is really the case when you feel like that?*

PRAY ABOUT IT

Read Deuteronomy 31 v 6. Thank God that He has promised to never leave His people. Thank Him that Jesus guarantees that all believers are safe with Him forever.

→ TAKE IT FURTHER

Goodbye! Please drop by page 109.

8 | God vs Dagon

The Israelites were defeated by the Philistines, who stole the ark of the covenant. God's glory left Israel. Now the action switches to the Philistines — surely life is now great for them.

👁 Read 1 Samuel 5 v 1–5

ENGAGE YOUR BRAIN

▷ Where did they keep the ark? (v2)

▷ What happened? (v3)

▷ And the next day? (v4)

The Philistines worshipped false god Dagon and assumed he was way stronger than God. They got a wake-up call the next two mornings about who was the true God. Dagon bowed down before the Lord! And God hadn't finished with the Philistines...

👁 Read verses 6–12

▷ What happened to the people of Ashdod? (v6)

▷ What did they recognise? (v7)

▷ What happened in Gath? (v9)

▷ And in Ekron? (v10–12)

The Philistines thought the precious ark had fallen into their hands, but actually they had fallen into God's hands. They worshipped false gods and not the Lord, so He showed them His devastating power. The Philistines realised God's ark was responsible for all their suffering and their god Dagon could do nothing about it.

GET ON WITH IT

▷ What idols do you have?

▷ What gets far more of your respect and attention than God?

▷ How will you kick these idols out of your life?

PRAY ABOUT IT

Talk these things over with God.

THE BOTTOM LINE

God alone deserves our worship. He is unbeatably powerful.

→ TAKE IT FURTHER

Handy tips on page 109.

11

9 | Raiders of the lost ark

The Philistines are regretting stealing the ark from the Israelites. God has struck them down with a nasty plague. They can't get rid of the ark soon enough.

👁 Read 1 Samuel 6 v 1–12

ENGAGE YOUR BRAIN

▷ What did the Philistines send along with the ark? (v4, v7)

▷ What did they hope this would achieve? (v5)

Imagine making statues of tumours and rats! Out of gold! But these guys were not joking — they were desperate to please God, get rid of the ark, and hopefully God would stop punishing them. They remembered what happened when the Egyptians treated God badly (v6).

👁 Read 1 Sam 6 v 13 – 7 v 1

▷ How did the Israelites in Beth Shemesh react when they saw the ark? (v13)

▷ But what spoiled the party? (v19)

▷ Why did this happen?

▷ What did this show? (v20)

The ark was where God was present among His people. No one could look at it and expect to live. That's why it was usually covered. God is perfect and holy. We can't expect to go into His presence and survive.

And yet Jesus solved this problem for us. His death was the ultimate sacrifice and has made it possible for us to go safely into God's presence. But we must remember how holy and perfect and awesome God is. And how much He hates sin. God is not to be messed with.

THINK IT THROUGH

▷ Do you give God the respect He deserves?

▷ In what ways do you need to take God more seriously?

THE BOTTOM LINE

We must not take God lightly.

→ TAKE IT FURTHER

Make a raid on page 109.

10 ¦ Just do it ¦

The disaster of losing God's ark and the deadly reminder of treating it carelessly were beginning to turn God's people back to Him again.

👁 Read 1 Samuel 7 v 1–6

ENGAGE YOUR BRAIN
▷ *What did the Israelites do after the ark was returned? (v2)*
▷ *What action would show they were serious about returning to God? (v3)*
▷ *What would be the result? (end of v3)*
▷ *What did the people do? (v4, v6)*

It looked as if Israel was serious about serving God this time. They were genuinely upset for turning away from God. But an emotional response wasn't enough. Samuel told them that if they were serious about returning to God then they needed to prove it. This meant ditching all their other gods, statues and idols. God must be the only one they worship.

When we realise how much we've sinned against God, it's right to feel rotten and say sorry to Him. But real repentance isn't merely emotional. It must be backed up by action — a real change. If you want to live for God alone, then you must throw away anything that's more important to you than Him. And you must actually start serving Him — learning from His word, talking to Him, showing love for others etc. Don't just say sorry to God — prove you mean it!

GET ON WITH IT
▷ *Have you got rid of the idols in your life yet?*
▷ *What do you still need to do?*
▷ *And what positive things do you need to start doing as part of living for God?*

PRAY ABOUT IT
It's time to get honest with God. Talk to Him about how you've treated Him, the things you struggle with and how you need to change. And ask Him to help you. He will!

→ TAKE IT FURTHER
Just do it — turn to page 110.

13

11 │ Philistines attack... again

The Israelites have turned back to God. But would they still trust Him and serve Him when the terrifying Philistines attacked?

Read 1 Samuel 7 v 7–9

ENGAGE YOUR BRAIN

▶ How were the people feeling? (v7)

▶ So what did they do? (v8)

▶ And what did God do? (v9)

This was a big change. Before, they had hoped the ark would save them, like a lucky charm. This time they cried out to God to save them, trusting Him to fight for them.

Read verses 10–14

▶ What did God do for His people? (v10–11)

▶ How did Samuel commemorate God's victory? (v12)

▶ What was the great result for Israel? (v13–14)

Read verses 15–17

▶ What was Samuel's role in Israel?

Samuel had been called and equipped by God to keep the Israelites in a right relationship with God. He just about managed that, as judge, prophet and priest. But what would happen when Samuel died? Who would lead God's people? You'll have to wait and see...

Before, Israel had been ignoring God and it led to disaster. Now they were trusting in Him — look at the difference! The same is true for us. There are two ways to live and they have two very different outcomes.

▶ Which way are you living?

PRAY ABOUT IT

Pray that you will live for God and depend on Him as the most important thing in your life.

THE BOTTOM LINE

Choose God. Choose life.

→ TAKE IT FURTHER

Choose Take it further on page 110.

12 | Dare to be different

Life was great for Israel with Samuel as judge.
But he was getting old. And his sons were too corrupt
to be good leaders. And the Israelites were no longer
so happy living God's way. It all spelled trouble.

👁 Read 1 Samuel 8 v 1–9

ENGAGE YOUR BRAIN

▷ What was the people's response to Samuel's dishonest sons? (v5)
▷ Why do you think Samuel was annoyed? (v6)
▷ But who were they really rejecting? (v7)

Israel's leaders wanted the country to be safe and secure. But they'd failed to learn that the reason for their defeats wasn't the lack of a king — it was their own rejection of God and lack of trust in Him. This request was a foolish attempt to by-pass God.

👁 Read verses 10–22

▷ What would happen if Israel had a king? (v11–17)
▷ What would it lead to? (v18)
▷ Why did they want a king? (v20)
▷ What did God do with their disobedient request? (v22)

The people ignored God's warnings and demanded a king. They wanted their own way; they wanted to be like the people around them. So God gave them what they wanted. Sometimes God lets us have our own way so we learn that His way is always best.

THINK IT THROUGH

▷ In what ways do you want your own way and not God's?
▷ How do you want to fit in with people around you?
▷ Who do you most want to please?
▷ Are you prepared to live God's way and be different from the crowd?

PRAY ABOUT IT

Talk these things through with God.

→ TAKE IT FURTHER

For something different, try page 110.

Isn't the Bible irrelevant?

Each issue in TRICKY, we tackle those mind-bendingly difficult questions that confuse us all, as well as questions that friends bombard us with to catch us off guard. This time — isn't the Bible irrelevant these days?

A RELEVANT BOOK

When I bought my car (one which actually accelerates when you ask it to, an improvement on my previous car), it came with a manual. The manual's great: it's been written to tell me everything I need to know about the car, and it's been written by Peugeot, who built the car. It's a massively relevant book; I'd be foolish not to use it.

AN IRRELEVANT BOOK?

It's a common belief that the Bible is a book which is out of date, out of touch, irrelevant. Maybe you think that way; you'll certainly have friends who do. But let's think about why the Bible was written, and who it's written by.

The Bible is clear that it's been written for two main purposes.

- *"The Scriptures ... are able to make you wise for salvation through faith in Christ Jesus"* (2 Timothy 3 v 15). The Scriptures (we tend to call them "the Bible") tell us how we can be saved for eternal life by trusting in Jesus Christ.

- *"All Scripture ... is useful for teaching, rebuking, correcting and training in righteousness, so that the man of God may be thoroughly equipped for every good work"* (2 Timothy 3 v 16–17). The Bible tells God's people how they should live in God's world.

These things give the Bible great relevance, both for how we live today, and for how we view our future. Of course, my manual's only any use because it's written

it was when it was first written. It's how God speaks to us to tell us who we are, what our future holds, how life works. There's no book more relevant!

WHO KNOWS BEST?

But in the 21st century, can't we work out for ourselves how to run our countries, our relationships, and our social lives? On some issues, don't we know better than God? That seems a good argument... until you pick up a newspaper or look around you and see the broken states, broken hearts, and broken bodies caused by ignoring what God says. Maybe human society doesn't know best after all.

The Bible often speaks of something called "blessing". To be blessed is to live as we were made to, knowing real satisfaction and security. The blessed life is the best life. And Psalm 1 tells us that the blessed person *"does not walk in the counsel of the wicked"* (v1), acting on the advice of a society which thinks God is irrelevant. Instead their *"delight is in the law of the LORD, and meditate on his law day and night"* (v2). Security and satisfaction — the best life — is based on reading, hearing, remembering and following the Bible.

by the car's maker; and the Bible is important because it is written by the world's Maker. *"All Scripture is God-breathed"* (2 Timothy 3 v 16): the Bible is the way God speaks to us.

LIVING AND ACTIVE

"The word of God is living and active" (Hebrews 4 v 12). This world is still the world God made, just as much as when the Bible was written. And the Bible's writer is still exactly the same as when the Bible was written; Jesus, God's Son, *"is the same yesterday and today and forever"* (Hebrews 13 v 8). The word of God is living, not dead; up-to-date not out-of-date. It's as relevant to today's world as

My car works best when I consult the maker's words. Our lives work best, and work eternally, if we realise our Maker's words are not irrelevant, but are *"more precious than gold"* (Psalm 19 v 10).

17

2 Thessalonians

Ready, steady, grow

When Paul and Silas first visited the city of Thessalonica (now in Greece), it had been an eye-opening experience. Paul told people about Jesus and many became Christians. But the local Jews were furious, started a riot and chased Paul and Silas out of town. Despite this opposition, the church grew in Thessalonica.

IS GOD FAIR?

This is Paul's second lettter to this group of Christians. It seems things were going well — the Christians were growing in faith and love and hanging in there despite the opposition. The trouble was, some of the Christians were getting tired of being persecuted and began to doubt if God was a fair God after all. If God's fair, why were they getting such a hard time for following Him?

WHERE'S JESUS?

Two other problems had cropped up too — some people were trying to con the Christians into thinking Jesus had already come back (yeah right, as if he could have booked into a hotel unnoticed).

WHY WORK?

And then there was the problem of work. Some of them seemed to think that if Jesus wasn't coming back soon, then there was no point working hard right now. But Paul soon shot these ideas down in flames.

In this letter, Paul gives the lowdown on God's justice, Jesus' return and working hard for God. It's all vital stuff for growing Christians, so let's start feasting on Paul's energy-giving words.

13 | Pray time

If you wrote a "top 3" list of things you pray about, what would be in there? Worries? Needs? School/work? Stuff that gets you down? Thanks to God? What about other Christians — how often do you pray for them?

👁 Read 2 Thess 1 v 1–4

ENGAGE YOUR BRAIN

ⓘ How did Paul and co. greet these Christians? (v2)

ⓘ What did they thank God for? (v3)

ⓘ What did they tell other people about this church? (v4)

Wouldn't it be great if people said these things about your church or youth group? Paul thanked God for the growing faith of these Christians. They were great at showing love for each other. And all of this despite suffering loads of persecution.

GET ON WITH IT

Start a prayer list. Right now. In a notebook, scribble the names of all the Christians you know. Yes, all of them. Every day, go down the list, taking the next 3 or 4 names and praying for them. Thank God for good things about them. Pray that their faith will grow, that they'll be more loving and that they'll stand firm in the face of persecution.

👁 Read verse 5

ⓘ What did these guys' faith and perseverance show about God?

ⓘ And what would it mean for them? (end of v5)

It seems that some people in the church questioned how fair God is. It didn't seem fair that they were persecuted so much. But these Christians were evidence of God's fairness. Yes they suffered, but God helped them to cope with it and used it to help them grow in faith and love.

PRAY ABOUT IT

Ask God to help you cope with any persecution you face. Ask Him to strenthen you so you grow in faith and love.

→ TAKE IT FURTHER

Fair's fair on page 110.

14 | Judge Jesus

Some Thessalonian Christians were saying: "It's not right, God. Life's so unfair sometimes." Ever felt the same? Well, you're not alone. These newish Christians wanted to know whether God cared. Why was life so unfair?

👁 Read 2 Thess 1 v 6–7

ENGAGE YOUR BRAIN

▷ *How will God treat people differently and why?*

▷ *When will this happen?*

Some of these guys thought that their suffering proved God was unfair. But God was using persecution to strengthen them. They would have to wait for Jesus to return as Judge before justice was completed.

👁 Read verses 8–10

▷ *Who will Jesus punish? (v8)*

▷ *What will happen to them? (v9)*

▷ *What will heaven be like? (v10)*

There's a big contrast in these verses between believers and unbelievers. Paul is pretty clear that those who don't know God or obey Jesus will be thrown out of God's presence. Forever. Terrifying.

But (eternal) life will be very different for believers. Those who truly love God will live with Jesus. Forever. God is fair and just — He will punish those who reject Him and reward those who live for Him.

PRAY ABOUT IT

Find your list from yesterday. Pick several Christians and thank God that they will live with Him forever. Now make another list, with the names of non-Christians you know. Pick several every day and pray that God would rescue them so they can spend eternity with Him.

THE BOTTOM LINE

Jesus will judge fairly.

→ TAKE IT FURTHER

No *Take it further* today, to give you extra time to pray.

15 | Talking to God

In this letter we get great glimpses into how Paul prayed. So let's listen to his words and then try it out ourselves.

👁 Read 2 Thess 1 v 11–12

ENGAGE YOUR BRAIN

▶ *What two things did Paul pray for these Christians? (v11)*

▶ *Why? (v12)*

Paul cares so much for these Christians — he wants them to stick at serving God and for God to do great things through them. And all this so that God gets the glory He deserves.

PRAY ABOUT IT

Let's get praying. First, list Christians who are having a tough time:
-
-
-
-
-
-

Pray that they'll keep going and that God will keep them close to Him and use them to serve Him.

Now list some more Christians you know — of varying ages:
-
-
-
-
-
-

Pray that God will "fulfil every good purpose of theirs and every act prompted by their faith". Pray specifically about some of the ways they serve God.

Finally, pray that in your life and the lives of all these Christians, Jesus will be glorified by what you say and do.

THE BOTTOM LINE

Pray for other Christians. Make sure Jesus is at the centre of your prayers.

→ TAKE IT FURTHER

More prayer stuff on page 110.

16 Man of lawlessness

The church at Thessalonica was buzzing with rumours that Jesus had returned. Paul wasn't sure where this rumour came from but he was determined to squash it.

👁 **Read 2 Thess 2 v 1–5**

ENGAGE YOUR BRAIN

🔘 *What will happen to God's people when Jesus returns? (v1)*

🔘 *Had it happened yet? (v3)*

🔘 *Who would show up first? (v3–4)*

The *man of lawlessness* is the antichrist, who will appear just before Jesus returns, claiming to be God. We don't know who he'll be, but he will deceive those who don't know Jesus.

👁 **Read verses 6–12**

🔘 *Who will defeat the antichrist? (v8)*

🔘 *What will happen when this evil man arrives? (v9)*

🔘 *What will happen to those who follow him? (v10–12)*

🔘 *Why? (v10)*

It will be extra tough for Christians just before Jesus returns. It's also hard for Christians now — Paul says the powers that try to drag us away from following Jesus are already at work (v7). But those who keep on trusting Jesus will be rescued (v10). So we don't need to worry. We just need to stand firm. More about that tomorrow.

PRAY ABOUT IT

This is all scary stuff. But thank God that He is in complete control; that He will look after His people for ever; that Jesus will return to defeat evil.

THE BOTTOM LINE

Be on your guard, but remember God's in control.

→ **TAKE IT FURTHER**

More scary stuff on page 111.

17 | Make a stand

These Christians had every reason to be miserable and terrified. They were persecuted for their beliefs and Paul had just told them all about the antichrist! But now Paul explains why they'll be OK.

👁 **Read 2 Thess 2 v 13–14**

ENGAGE YOUR BRAIN

▶ *What had God done for these believers?*
-
-
-

▶ *And what would this lead to? (end of v14)*

This is true for all Christians! We know we'll be safe for all eternity because God chose us from the beginning. He never changes — we can trust Him. The Holy Spirit works in us and makes us more like Jesus. And one day we'll share in His glory. No opposition or antichrist can stop that from happening!

👁 **Read verses 15–17**

▶ *So what should we do? (v15)*

▶ *How will Jesus help us along the way? (v16–17)*

Life will often be tough for Christians. But we must stand firm, keep going and hold on to the truth of the gospel. One way to do this would be to memorise some of these verses. And we can ask Jesus to encourage and strengthen us to worship Him in all that we say and do.

PRAY ABOUT IT

Use verses 16–17 to pray for yourself and for Christian friends.

THE BOTTOM LINE

Stand firm. Jesus will get you through.

→ TAKE IT FURTHER

Stand over there... on page 111.

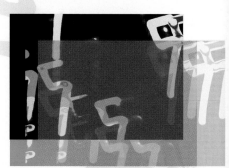

18 Paul's prayer pointers

It's time for another lesson from Paul on how to pray. Let's put it into action right away.

👁 Read 2 Thess 3 v 1–5

ENGAGE YOUR BRAIN

▷ What did Paul ask these believers to do? (v1)

▷ What should they pray for him? (v1–2)

▷ Why could they take courage during dark times? (v3)

▷ What did Paul ask God to do for them? (v5)

PRAY ABOUT IT

1. Think who you can ask to pray for you. Now email or text them with what you'd like them to pray for.

2. Pray for the gospel. Ask the Lord to spread the truth about Jesus. Pray for Christians you know — that they'll share the gospel more. And pray for people you know who need to hear and accept the message of Jesus.

3. Thank God for His faithfulness. Praise Him for what He's like.

4. Ask Him to strengthen you and protect you from the devil's attacks.

5. Pray for Christians you don't often pray for. Ask God to help them keep going in the faith and to become more loving and more like Jesus.

➔ TAKE IT FURTHER
Paul's obsession — page 111.

19 | Job slobs

On a scale of 1 to 10, how lazy are you? Do you use your time wisely? Do you work hard or take it easy? Do you expect parents or others to provide for you all the time? If so, watch out, Paul's on the war path...

👁 Read 2 Thess 3 v 6–15

ENGAGE YOUR BRAIN
🔘 Who were they to keep away from? (v6)

🔘 What do you think of Paul's rule in v10?

🔘 What should we never be too tired to do? (v13)

🔘 How were they to treat lazy Christians? (v14–15)

🔘 What gave Paul's instructions extra seriousness? (v6, v12)

Paul's not saying that if you're unemployed, you shouldn't be allowed any food to eat. Paul was talking to people who had work to do, but were not doing it. People who were avoiding responsibilities.

Christians should work hard for others, ready for Jesus' return. They should not expect a free ride and never be too tired to do good. In our work, we can glorify God.

👁 Read verses 16–18
🔘 Who can you pray v16 and v18 for?

GET ON WITH IT
🔘 In what ways are you lazy?
🔘 What specifically will you do to be a harder worker?
🔘 Who do you sponge from?
🔘 What specifically can you do to earn your way?

PRAY ABOUT IT
Talk to God about your attitudes to work and being provided for.

THE BOTTOM LINE
Work hard. Don't be a sponger.

➡ TAKE IT FURTHER
The final word on 2 Thessalonians is on page 111.

What is the gospel?

In *Essential*, we take time out to explore key truths about God, the Bible and Christianity. At the heart of Christianity is a 6-letter word: the GOSPEL. It simply means "good news". But what is this good news? And why do we need it?

THE BAD NEWS

Human beings are in a mess. It's not just that we have bad hair days, fail exams and hurt the people we care about — we're in far deeper trouble than that.

God designed humans to live in relationship with Him — revelling in His love, enjoying His gifts and obeying His good rules (Genesis chapters 1–2). The first humans managed it for a while but then they decided to throw it all away. They chose to put themselves before God, they stopped trusting God and stopped living His way (Genesis 3 v 1–7).

That decision had massive consequences. Since that moment, every human being who has ever been born has been a rebel (Romans 5 v 18–19). We all naturally ignore God and this means that we end up thinking, saying and doing stuff that is very far from what He would want. This is what the Bible calls "sin". God is perfect and He is passionate about justice, so He won't ignore this sin. He has said that everyone who rebels deserves anger (Romans 1 v 18), separation from Him (Colossians 1 v 21) and death (Hebrews 9 v 27) — forever. Seriously bad news!

THE GOOD NEWS

But the bad news isn't the end of the story. Even before the first humans rebelled, God had a plan to sort out the mess. 2,000 years ago, He sent His Son, Jesus, into the world. And Jesus is the best news imaginable!

At the end of 3 years of preaching, teaching and performing miracles, Jesus was arrested. He was nailed to a cross and left to die. His physical

> For I am not ashamed of the gospel, because it is the power of God that brings salvation to everyone who believes: first to the Jew, then to the Gentile.
>
> Romans 1:16

suffering was horrific but it achieved something spectacular:

- When He hung on the cross, Jesus took the punishment we deserve for our rebellion. He faced God's anger so we don't have to. He made it possible for us to be forgiven all our sin (Romans 3 v 25).

- When He died, Jesus smashed the wall that separates us from God (Colossians 1 v 22), leaving us free to have a relationship with Him, free to become God's precious children.

- And when He rose again from the grave, Jesus conquered death and opened the way to eternal life (John 3 v 16). He's now in heaven, ruling the earth — one day He'll come back to judge the earth and take all His followers to the best place imaginable.

That's Jesus — the good news — the gospel. And if we let the truth of it sink in, it is mind-blowingly fantastic news! Jesus takes ordinary human beings like us and, even though we have done nothing to deserve it, He offers rebels a new start, outcasts a new family and condemned people new hope for the future. What an awesome God!

HEADLINE NEWS

This gospel is at the centre of Christianity. We become Christians by believing the good news and accepting that we need Jesus' forgiveness. We live as Christians by remembering the good news and putting Jesus first in everything we think, say and do. And we encourage other people to become Christians by explaining the good news and showing how brilliant Jesus is.

Ephesians 2 v 1–10 is a great summary of the gospel. Why not spend a few moments reading it now? Then thank Jesus for being the best news imaginable and ask Him to help you believe, remember and live out the gospel every day of your life...

Isaiah

City of dreams

Isaiah is one of the longest, weirdest and most challenging books in the Bible. It's all about Jerusalem, the city where God lived among His people. In Isaiah's time, Jerusalem was falling apart — God's people had rejected Him.

Isaiah goes into great detail about how God would rightly punish them. But he also tells us about God's rescue plan for those who stick with Him. And he outlines God's plans for a brand new Jerusalem — a perfect city at the centre of God's new heavens and earth. Here's how the book fits together...

Chapters 1–5: Rebellion
God's people disobey Him and are heading for God's punishment. But there are signs that God hasn't given up on them yet.

Chapters 6–12: Perfect King
In contrast with evil King Ahaz, God will raise up a ruler from King David's family who will reign forever.

Chapters 13–27: A coming day
God rules nations, and He shows it in acts of judgment that point us ahead to God's world-shaking final day.

Chapters 28–37: Undeserved rescue
God will punish His own people too, but amazingly, will show them mercy.

Chapters 38–55: Sinless servant
God will rescue people from exile and deal with their ongoing sin by sending someone to die in their place.

Chapters 56–66: Conquering hero
God's King will crush His enemies and launch a new creation. God's people will live with Him in a new Jerusalem.

This issue, we take in the first half of Isaiah. Come and expand your view of God, His plans and His chosen King, Jesus. And learn where you need to put your trust.

20 | Court in the act

There's no gentle beginning in Isaiah. The book explodes into action with God's people in the dock, accused of terrible crimes.

👁 Read Isaiah 1 v 1–9

ENGAGE YOUR BRAIN

▶ *What does God accuse His people of doing? (v2–4)*
▶ *What happened to them because of their crimes? (v5–8)*
▶ *Was there any hope for the future? (v9)*

No wonder God sent other nations to punish His people. Frighteningly, even this heavy discipline didn't do the trick. The people of Judah still wouldn't turn back to God.

👁 Read verses 10–20

▶ *How did the people try to please God? (v10–20)*
▶ *Why did God hate this? (v15–16)*
▶ *So what should God's people actually do? (v16–17)*
▶ *What did God promise them if they went back to living His way? (v18–19)*
▶ *What was the alternative? (v20)*

Going through the motions and rituals won't please God. It means nothing if we're still living for ourselves and not God. People who truly live for God learn to do right, seek justice and stand up for those in need (v17). We've all sinned and deserve destruction, but those who stick with God have a great future — their sins will be wiped out and God will provide for them.

THINK IT OVER

▶ *Are you going through the motions or really living for God?*
▶ *What do you need to start doing right?*

PRAY ABOUT IT

Talk these things through with God. Thank Him that even though we've rejected Him, He gives us the chance to have our sins wiped out, because of Jesus and His death for us.

➡ TAKE IT FURTHER

Meet four kings on page 111.

21 | Pure punishment

"Purifying" sounds like a such a nice, gentle idea. But to purify something (like gold or water) involves a tough process which gets rid of any dirt or bad stuff. The same goes for God purifying His "dirty" people.

Read Isaiah 1 v 21–31

▶ What were God's people once like? (v21)

▶ What had they become? (v21–23)

▶ How would God purify them? (v25)

▶ What would they become? (v26)

The people of Judah refused to turn back to God, so He would punish them. The big surprise is that He wouldn't wipe them out — He would purify them and keep them as His people. Far, far better than they deserved. But it wouldn't be easy.

Metal ore passes through fire on its way to becoming pure metal; and God's people would be purified by the fire of His judgment, punishing them and rooting out everything and everyone that was impure.

Read verses 27–31

▶ What were the two ways to live and their consequences? (v27–28)

God would redeem His people — rescue them, buy them back. It would cost the life of His Son, Jesus.

All the talk of sacred trees and gardens in v29–31 is referring to idol worship and false religion. These disgusting places and the people who did such things would be destroyed.

PRAY ABOUT IT

Thank God that He longs to purify us. If you're a Christian, praise Him for sending His Son to rescue you. If you're still unsure about it all, ask God to make it clear to you and show you the seriousness of rejecting Him.

THE BOTTOM LINE

God purifies His people.

→ TAKE IT FURTHER

Pure gold on page 112.

22 | Futuristic city

God's people in Jerusalem continued to reject Him so He would punish them but also purify them. Next, Isaiah tells us how Jerusalem was meant to be. The ideal city of God.

👁 Read Isaiah 2 v 1–5

ENGAGE YOUR BRAIN

⚪ What will happen to Jerusalem "in the last days"? (v2)

⚪ What will God do for His people? (v3)

This is what God's city was meant to be like — God's people living with Him as King, obeying His word, living His way and drawing in others who wanted to live God's way too. The great news is that this *will* happen.

⚪ What else will God do for people? (v4)

⚪ How will nations change the way they relate to each other?

⚪ What are God's people called to do? (v5)

Israel, God's people, were to be a light to the godless nations around them. They should be attracted by what they saw of Israel living the good life with God in control. In reality, Israel often lived more like these evil nations. But Isaiah looks forward to a day when God's people will again be a light, attracting the nations to God's kingdom.

SHARE IT

⚪ How do non-believers view you and the way you live?

⚪ How can you be a bright light to those around you?

⚪ How can you draw people into God's kingdom?

PRAY ABOUT IT

Pray for opportunities to show people the way to Jesus. And pray about conflict in the world today (v4). Thank God that one day He'll bring peace to all nations.

→ TAKE IT FURTHER

Follow the light to page 112.

23 Pulverising pride

Yesterday Isaiah told us about a day when God's city will be raised up, people will flock there and God will bring peace to the nations. But now Isaiah tells us what will happen to people who live for themselves, rejecting God.

👁 Read Isaiah 2 v 6–11

▷ *What was Israel full of?*
v6:
v7:
v8:
▷ *So what would happen to them? (v9)*
▷ *What should they fear? (v10)*

The Israelites were rich and also had a mighty army, but they were superstitious and worshipped idols. They relied on themselves and false religion rather than on the one true God. They were full of pride and so God would humble them. Only He would be raised up (v11).

👁 Read verses 12–22

▷ *What will happen to the wealth and idols they relied on? (v20)*
▷ *What word of warning does Isaiah leave us with? (v22)*

In v13–16, Isaiah lists some of the greatest things of his day — they would all be humbled on the day of the Lord. And everyone who chased wealth, relied on their own strength or worshipped false gods would see what a terrible mistake they'd made. They would see how incredibly impressive and powerful the Lord is. The message is clear — *"stop trusting in man"*.

GET ON WITH IT

▷ *How do you rely on yourself rather than trusting in God?*
▷ *What do you worship more than God?*
▷ *What can you do to change this?*

PRAY ABOUT IT

Ask God to give you a healthy fear of His day of judgment. Pray that this fear would motivate you to turn away from pride and worshipping the wrong things, and to trust in Christ's death for you.

THE BOTTOM LINE

Stop trusting in man.

➡ TAKE IT FURTHER

No *Take it further* section today.

24 Leaders or losers?

What do you think of your country's leaders? What do you imagine God thinks of them? Well, He didn't have a good word to say about Israel's leaders, who had led them away from God.

👁 Read Isaiah 3 v 1–15

ENGAGE YOUR BRAIN

▶ *What would happen to Israel's leaders and who would replace them? (v1–7)*

▶ *Why? (v8–9, v11)*

▶ *What about those who still lived God's way? (v10)*

Israel's leaders had ruined God's people. They'd been greedy, oppressed the poor, and trusted in their own wealth and military power. So God would bring them down and Israel would be ruled by children. They would get what they deserved for abandoning God.

👁 Read Isaiah 3 v 16 – 4 v 1

▶ *Why was Isaiah critical of these women? (v16)*

▶ *What had they relied on and been proud of? (v17–24)*

▶ *What would it be replaced with? (v17–24)*

▶ *And what about the warriors they relied on for protection?*

What was the big problem?

Pride – Fashion very easily becomes a way of being superior to those who just aren't cool.

Flirting – Clothes can be used to tantalise. But with all the men lost in battle, the flirts would be desperate for a husband (4 v 1).

Obsession – The list of accessories they'd lose (v18–23) shows they were obsessed with looking good.

▶ *Does fashion or your appearance ever take over your thoughts and priorities?*

PRAY ABOUT IT

Pray for leaders — of your nation and your church — that they would honour God in the decisions they make. And talk to God about your attitude to clothes and appearance.

→ TAKE IT FURTHER

Beauty tips are on page 112.

25 Branching out

Isaiah seems to regularly switch between good news and bad news. Yesterday we heard about the fate of Israel's useless leaders and fashion junkies. Today we're given a ray of hope. Well, a branch of hope.

Read Isaiah 4 v 2

ENGAGE YOUR BRAIN
▶ How is the Branch described?

▶ Who do you think Isaiah is talking about?

It's all about family trees. King David was known as the *Branch of Jesse* (his dad). So the *Branch of the Lord* is the promised King that God would send. Israel's leaders had failed, but one day God would send Jesus to restore pride and glory back to God's people.

Read verses 3–6
▶ How will God deal with Israel's sin? (v3–4)

▶ And what else would God provide for His people? (v5–6)

God would clean up Jerusalem and His people's sin (v4). When God rescued the Israelites from Egypt, He sent a pillar of cloud by day and one of fire by night, to guide and protect them and show that God was with them. Isaiah says God would once again guide and protect His people. Despite their sin, God made amazing promises to His people.

At the beginning of Isaiah, it looked as if it was all over for Jerusalem and God's people. They had continuously rejected and sinned in the most hideous ways. And so God promised to punish them, yet He would also purify them and give them the perfect leader to bring safety and glory back to God's city.

PRAY ABOUT IT
Read verse 2 again, thinking how it came true in Jesus. Spend time thanking God for sending His Son.

→ TAKE IT FURTHER
Time for Christmas! Page 112.

26 | Sad love song

Do you like love songs, or do you find them too cheesy?
Well, you won't have heard a love song like this before.
It's a song to God and features a vineyard, a watchtower
and some major hedge destruction.

👁 **Read Isaiah 5 v 1–2**

ENGAGE YOUR BRAIN

▷ *Who do you think the vineyard owner is?*

▷ *What shows how much he cared for it?*

▷ *Yet what happened? (end of v2)*

Now look ahead to verse 7 to discover who the vineyard owner is and who the vineyard represents.

👁 **Read verses 3–7**

▷ *What more could God have done for His people?*

▷ *Yet how did they respond? (v4, 7)*

▷ *So what was the verdict? (v5–6)*

God had done everything He could for His people, yet they responded disgustingly (we'll read all about their "bad fruit" tomorrow). God had done so much for them and so expected

justice and right living from them. Instead, He saw violence and distress.

But let's not look down on the Israelites for the way they treated God. We need to make sure we don't do the same. God's done even more for us — He sent His Son to die for us and rescue us. And if we respond as the Israelites did, then we deserve destruction too.

PRAY ABOUT IT

Thank God that He gives us far more than we deserve. Pray that you'll be fruitful in serving Him and other Christians.

THE BOTTOM LINE

God cares for you. Don't throw His love back in His face.

➔ **TAKE IT FURTHER**

Another vine mess on page 112.

27 | The name of the woes

God's people were like a vineyard who produced rotten, stinking fruit, despite all the care God had shown them. Today we find out exactly what they'd been doing. By the way, woe = punishment.

👁 Read Isaiah 5 v 8–19

ENGAGE YOUR BRAIN

▷ *What had they done wrong?*
v8:
v11–12:
v18:

▷ *How would God punish them?*
v9–10:
v13–15:

▷ *How is the Lord described? (v16)*

👁 Read verses 20–25

▷ *What had they done wrong?*
v20:
v21:
v22–23:

▷ *How would God punish them?*
(v24–25)

👁 Read verses 26–30

▷ *What would God do? (v26–28)*

▷ *What would happen to God's people? (v29–30)*

God's people would be conquered and taken away by invading armies (first the Assyrians, then the Babylonians). These were Israel's enemies. Yet, because of Israel's sin, God would command these nations to defeat His people.

THINK IT OVER

It's easy to read these verses and jab a finger at Israel and think: "We're not as bad as that". Think twice.

▷ *How does God view those who know of Him but reject Him?*

It all sounds horrible. But tomorrow we'll discover that God wasn't giving up on His people.

PRAY ABOUT IT

Which of the six woes could be applied to you? Ask God to help you deal with anything that gets in the way of your relationship with Him.

➔ TAKE IT FURTHER

Woe, woe, woe the boat to p113.

28 | The perfect King

God's people had cut themselves off from Him and earned His severe punishment (chapters 1–5). This is the situation in which Isaiah was sent to be God's messenger to the people. But Isaiah didn't send an application for the job...

👁 Read Isaiah 6 v 1–4

ENGAGE YOUR BRAIN

▶ *King Uzziah ruled Judah for 52 years. Impressive. But who's the real king? (v1)*

▶ *How did the seraphs ("burning ones") show their respect for God? (v2)*

▶ *What big truth about God did they shout? (v3)*

👁 Read verses 5–7

▶ *How did Isaiah respond to the sight of perfect, holy God on His throne? (v5)*

▶ *What did he confess? (v5)*

▶ *So what did God do for Isaiah? (v6–7)*

Isaiah didn't say "Wow! Amazing!" or "Where's my camera?" His reaction was complete terror. He knew he was too sinful to be in the presence of God. But God provides a way for Isaiah to be made clean (v6–7).

Sometimes we think that a small sin isn't that bad. Or we ask if it's fair for God to punish sin with hell. But maybe our problem is that we haven't grasped how pure and holy God is and how disgusting sin is to Him.

God didn't ignore Isaiah's sin, He dealt with it. This happened on the altar, where sacrifices to God were put. This hints at how God would deal with sin for good — Jesus would be sacrificed on the cross to "atone" (cover) our sin, if we trust Him to.

PRAY ABOUT IT

Thank God for the vision of His holiness and glory which Isaiah saw. Thank Him that we clearly see His glory and holiness in Jesus Christ, who sacrificed Himself for us, so that our sin can be cleaned up.

→ TAKE IT FURTHER

Seeing God — page 113.

29 | Send me! Send me!

Isaiah saw a vision of God on His throne. When he saw God's perfection, Isaiah felt so dirty and sinful. But God took away Isaiah's sin and gave him a mission.

👁 Read Isaiah 6 v 8–10

ENGAGE YOUR BRAIN

▶ *What was Isaiah's brilliant answer to God's question?*

▶ *What was surprising about the message he'd tell the people?*

Not only would people not respond to God but He'd harden their hearts as punishment for rejecting Him. God's people had chosen to go their own way, ignoring God, so the Lord would give them exactly what they'd chosen — life without Him, unable to understand the truth.

👁 Read verses 11–13

▶ *What would happen to Judah? (v11–12)*

▶ *But what hope was there? (v13)*

No wonder Isaiah's book is so long — He had to keep taking God's message to His people until the whole country was in ruins. Not an easy or happy

task. Yet Isaiah was willing to do it (v8). And there was a glimmer of hope — a few faithful people would remain after all this devastation.

This is all a picture of the world's fate. History will end in God's judgment, caused by people's refusal to accept the gospel — the message of Jesus. But not everyone will be wiped out — Jesus will rescue those who trust in Him.

GET ON WITH IT

▶ *Are you as enthusiastic about serving God as Isaiah was?*
▶ *What jobs for God have you been avoiding?*
▶ *How will you respond enthusiastically?*

PRAY ABOUT IT

Ask God to fill you with enthusiasm for serving Him, however tough the task seems.

TAKE IT FURTHER

Sending you to page 113.

30 | Ignoring God

Isaiah's mission: to tell God's people that anyone who refused to trust God would become hardened so they could never trust Him. Now we see that actually happening with King Ahaz.

👁 Read Isaiah 7 v 1–9

ENGAGE YOUR BRAIN

▷ *What was the crisis for Ahaz, king of Judah? (v1–2)*

▷ *What was God's message to Ahaz? (v4, v9)*

Aram (AKA Syria) and Israel (AKA Ephraim) got together against superpower Assyria and tried to bully Ahaz into joining them. But God told Ahaz to forget about politics and trust God to rescue His people. Ahaz refused, so God spoke again.

👁 Read verses 10-17

▷ *What did God want Ahaz to do? (v11)*

▷ *But what did He do? (v12)*

God's angry response (v13–17) sounds weird but it was a picture message. The virgin (God's people) would give birth to a son (a faithful remnant who trusted God) and God would be with them. But Ahaz (and anyone who refused God's help) would face God's punishment. Verse 14 points us forward to Jesus (*Immanuel*) who'd be born as a human baby — He would be God living with His people.

👁 Read verses 18–25

Ahaz refused God's help so Judah would face the consequences. No one and no part of the land would escape God's judgment.

THINK IT OVER

"If you do not stand firm in your faith, you will not stand at all."

▷ *Where have you placed your trust?*

PRAY ABOUT IT

Ask God to help you to keep calm and not be afraid when faced with a crisis. Ask His help to keep trusting in Him, not refusing His help.

→ TAKE IT FURTHER

More Jesus stuff on page 113.

31 Tongue-twisting tot

"Isaiah and his wife would like to announce the birth at 2pm on Tuesday of Maher-Shalal-Hash-Baz." Yes, that really was his name. A good choice? Well, it was God's choice — let's find out why.

Read Isaiah 8 v 1–10

ENGAGE YOUR BRAIN

- *Have you got a footnote in your Bible explaining what this crazy name means?*
- *Why was he called that? (v4)*
- *What was this "flood" that would destroy Israel and Judah? (v7)*
- *Why did God send it against His people? (v6)*

The tongue-twisting name Maher-Shalal-Hash-Baz means *"Quick to the plunder, swift to the spoil"*. It was a promise that Judah's enemies would be defeated, and an invitation to trust in God. But Judah rejected God's invitation (that's what v6 means), and so He would send Assyria to wash away His rebellious people.

Read verses 11–22

- *How was Isaiah to be different from the rest of His nation? (v12)*
- *What was Isaiah's decision? (v17)*
- *Who shouldn't we listen to? (v19)*
- *Where should we turn for guidance? (v19–20)*

Many people choose to trust in schemes, conspiracies or fortune tellers rather than God. They fear humans instead of the Lord. But we should be like Isaiah: trusting God; fearing Him and His judgment; obeying His word and waiting for Jesus to return.

THINK IT OVER

- *Where do you wrongly put your trust sometimes?*
- *What do you fear more than God?*
- *How will you change your thinking and living?*

PRAY ABOUT IT

You should have loads to talk to God about today.

THE BOTTOM LINE

Trust, fear and obey God.

TAKE IT FURTHER

There's more on page 113.

32 | A new dawn

This bit of Isaiah gets read in church at Christmas every year. It sounds so familiar, but it's message is awesome and revolutionary.

👁 **Read Isaiah 9 v 1–5**

ENGAGE YOUR BRAIN

▷ *What was the good news for these areas that would suffer vicious enemy attacks? (v1–2)*

▷ *What would happen to war, oppression and slavery? (v4–5)*

God promised a brilliant reversal of fortune for His people — starting in the part of the land which Assyria would invade first (v1). A new light will dawn for God's troubled people. Their distress will turn to joy; cruelty and war will end. God will be their King again, bring peace and justice.

👁 **Read verses 6–7**

▷ *Who is this talking about? (v6–7)*

▷ *How is He described? Put v6 into your own words:*

▷ *What will this King's reign be like? (v7)*

God's people have a great future because of this baby, who would be the perfect King — Jesus Christ. This is revolutionary stuff: He will overthrow cruel regimes and rule with justice and righteousness. Yes, God will ruthlessly punish sin, but look at the incredible future for those who trust in Him!

PRAY ABOUT IT

Go through verses 6–7, phrase by phrase, turning them into a prayer (or song!) of praise to King Jesus.

➔ **TAKE IT FURTHER**

More from Matthew on page 114.

Christians and music

Music is an amazing part of God's creation. It has the power to fill us with joy or make us cry. It can be relaxing, exciting, uplifting or even alarming. Music is everywhere. Even the Bible is full of songs.

MUSIC IN THE BIBLE

At all the major points of the Bible story, God's people sing. Think about Moses and the Israelites crossing the Red Sea as God rescues them from Egypt (Exodus 15), the birth of the last judge (Hannah's song in 1 Samuel 2), the whole book of Psalms. Or how about Mary when she's told she will give birth to the Son of God (Luke 1)? Ultimately all creation will join in singing God's praise — just flick through the book of Revelation to see God's people gathered round His throne in heaven.

MUSIC IN OUR HEADPHONES

But what about the music we listen to now? Does it have to be Christian music? What do we fill our ears and our minds with? Take a minute to think through what's on your current playlist. Did you pick the tracks because they're by a band you like,

or because a friend recommended them or you heard it on the radio and liked it? What about the lyrics? Stop reading this for a minute and listen to them, really listen...

MOTIVE AND MESSAGE

When you listen to a track, there are two helpful things to have in mind: motive and message. Motive — why do they write/perform? Some artists write songs simply to make money, others to express their views, and others to explore reality. And what's the message? What worldview are they promoting? Does it fit with a biblical view of things?

How about that track you just listened to? What's the motive and message? There is a lot of music out there and a lot of it is great, but equally there is some that can tempt us to sin in the way we think and act. Or even lead us away from God. Here are some helpful Bible bits to inform what we choose to put on our playlist.

- **Philippians 4 v 8**
  Does this describe your music?

- **1 Corinthians 10 v 23**
  There are no rules in the Bible about what we should and shouldn't listen to, but do your music choices glorify God as positive expressions of human creative talent? Or are they promoting things that twist and spoil God's good gifts?

- **1 Corinthians 15 v 33**
  Don't be naive. If you fill your head with lyrics full of bad language and bad morals, it's going to affect what you think and say.

MUSIC DILEMMAS

So what do you do when you realise your latest favourite tune has lyrics which talk about women in an over-sexualised way? Do you keep the song? Or what if your friend asks you to make them a playlist and gives you a list of songs, but one has explicit lyrics? What do you say? How about if you're at a music festival and everyone's heading to the main stage to hear a great band who are popular but are known for their obscene lyrics? What do you do?

You might find some of these situations easier to deal with than others. But they can all lead to positive opportunities. Remember that Jesus prayed this for his disciples: *"My prayer is not that you take them out of the world but that you protect them from the evil one"* (John 17 v 15). Sometimes we can use these dilemmas as an opportunity to share our faith and worldview.

MUSIC CHOICE

So be wise; know yourself — what will encourage you in your faith and what will make it harder for you to avoid sinning? What's worth celebrating in human musical creativity and what's not? Use your brain as well as your ears and ask God to help you be discerning.

And finally, don't forget that there is a lot of great Christian music out there too. We can nourish our souls with awesome lyrics about our Saviour, Lord and King — from mainstream praise music to great Christian rap and hiphop or RnB. http://www.crossrhythms.co.uk is one place to find them. Happy listening!

43

33 1 Samuel: Tall Saul's call

Let's get back to 1 Samuel. The Israelites were still not satisfied and demanded a king of their own, just like the other nations. But who would be chosen to be Israel's first king?

👁 Read 1 Samuel 9 v 1–17

ENGAGE YOUR BRAIN

▶ What was impressive about Saul? (v2)
▶ Why did Saul and his servant want to meet Samuel? (v6)
▶ But what had God told Samuel? (v16)
▶ Why would God give His people a king? (end of v16)

👁 Read verses 18-24

▶ What three pieces of surprising news did Samuel have for Saul? (v19–20)
▶ Why did Saul not believe he could be special to Israel? (v21)

Saul was looking for some lost donkeys, but instead he found God's prophet, who had some surprising news for him. Samuel claimed that Saul and his family were important to Israel. Saul was from an unimpressive family in the smallest Israelite tribe — how could *he* possibly be important??

Things like status aren't important to God. It didn't matter that Saul was from a lowly family — God would still use Saul to lead His people. God often uses weak people and surprising methods in His perfect plans.

THINK IT OVER

Ever think you're too unimportant or boring or bad to serve God in big ways? Think again. God uses all of His people in His plans — even weirdos like us.

PRAY ABOUT IT

Thank God that He's in control and can use us no matter how weak we are. Ask the Lord to show you how He wants to use you in His plans.

THE BOTTOM LINE

God can use anyone in His plans.

→ TAKE IT FURTHER

No *Take it further* section today.

34 | Time of the signs

Saul was looking for his dad's donkeys, but instead, found God's prophet, Samuel. Sam had some surprising news for Saul which would change his life for ever.

👁 Read 1 Sam 9 v 25 – 10 v 7

ENGAGE YOUR BRAIN

▶ What did Samuel announce in his secret ceremony with Saul? (v1)

▶ What signs that this was true did Samuel promise Saul?
v2:
v3–4:
v5–6:

▶ What other good news did Samuel have for Saul? (v7)

Pouring oil on Saul's head was a sign that God had chosen him to be king. He would rule over the Lord's inheritance — the Israelites and their land. And he would have God's support in everything he did for God.

👁 Read verses 8-16

▶ What was Samuel's final instruction to Saul? (v8)

▶ How did God change Saul? (v9–10)

▶ But what did Saul keep quiet about? (v16)

God gave Saul the Holy Spirit to help him, and Samuel would also instruct Saul how to serve the Lord.

God gives all His people (Christians) the Holy Spirit to help them serve Him. And He instructs us how to live for Him — the Bible is packed full of great advice on living God's way. We should read it, take it to heart and follow it.

PRAY ABOUT IT
Read Psalm 32 v 6–8 and use it to spur you on as you praise God.

→ TAKE IT FURTHER
Follow the signs to page 114.

35 | King of the luggage

God's people demanded to have their own king. Amazingly, God didn't destroy them for rejecting Him as king; He gave them what they asked for.

👁 Read 1 Sam 10 v 17–19

ENGAGE YOUR BRAIN

▷ *What did God remind His people about? (v18)*

▷ *But how had they treated God? (v19)*

Even though the Lord had rescued Israel again and again, they didn't want Him in charge. They wanted to be like other nations around them, with their own king to lead them into battle.

👁 Read verses 20–27

▷ *Why do you think Saul hid?*

▷ *How did the people react to their new king? (v24)*

▷ *Was Saul popular with everyone? (v27)*

The people were impressed with their new king because he was tall and looked impressive. But that wasn't

enough. Saul was God's chosen king, so he'd have to follow God's rules (v25). Israel now had a king, but God would still be charge.

If you're a Christian, you're one of God's people. He's in charge of your life. You live for Him. And He's given you His instructions (in the Bible) to help you serve Him and live for Him.

PRAY ABOUT IT

If you're serious about serving God, try this — every morning, ask God to help you live His way that day. Talk to Him about the day ahead. Hand over your worries to Him. Rely on Him.

→ TAKE IT FURTHER

King things on page 114.

46

36 Eye-opening stuff

Tall Saul had been chosen as Israel's first king. God was on his side, but there were still people who doubted Saul could rescue Israel from their violent enemies. It's time for a fight.

👁 Read 1 Samuel 11 v 1–5

ENGAGE YOUR BRAIN
- *What condition did nasty Nahash put in the peace treaty? (v2)*
- *How did the people of Jabesh Gilead respond? (v3)*
- *How do you think Saul will react to the news?*

Jabesh Gilead was an Israelite town, so its people were God's people. Nahash and the Ammonites were enemies of God and His people. It was a desperate situation. Could farmer Saul do anything about it?

👁 Read verses 6–11

- *How did Saul react to the news?*
- *How do we know Saul was God's chosen king? (v6)*
- *How did the Israelites respond? (v7–8)*
- *How successful was the dawn raid? (v11)*

Now no one was in doubt that Saul was God's choice as king. God's Spirit came to Saul, giving him power to do incredible things. With the support of the Israelites, Saul crushed Nahash and the Ammonites, rescuing Jabesh Gilead. Saul's first victory as king, and God was behind it.

What an amazing transformation. One minute Saul was a regular farmer, the next he was God's furious king, leading God's people to victory in battle. The Holy Spirit transformed Saul and enabled him to serve God in a powerful way.

PRAY ABOUT IT
Ever feel too useless or sinful to be any use to God? The great news for Christians is that God gives us His Holy Spirit to help us serve Him. Thank God for the wonderful gift of His Spirit. Ask God to give you the strength, courage and ability to serve Him this week.

→ TAKE IT FURTHER
More eye-opening stuff on page 114.

37 | Celebration nation

Saul has just led the Israelites to their finest victory since he became king. This silenced those who'd claimed Saul shouldn't be their king. But Saul's followers wanted to silence them permanently.

👁 Read 1 Sam 11 12–13

ENGAGE YOUR BRAIN

▷ *What did they want to do with these doubters?*

▷ *Why did Saul stop the executions?*

Saul showed compassion and forgiveness to those who'd doubted him. Just as God did with the Israelites when they'd turned their backs on Him, time after time. Saul seemed to be the sort of king God wanted — one who obeyed God's word and recognised it was God's victory. A promising start.

👁 Read verses 14–15

▷ *How would you describe the mood in Israel with their new king?*

So far, so great. All the Israelites got together and gave their allegiance to King Saul. More importantly, they renewed their commitment to living God's way.

We'll soon find out that Saul was far from the perfect king. But let's enjoy one of his finest hours — celebrating God's victory with God's people.

PRAY ABOUT IT

Thank God for sending Jesus to be the perfect King, showing amazing compassion and forgiving our sins.

→ TAKE IT FURTHER

A little background on page 114.

38 Faithful God

With Saul confirmed as king, the time was right for Sam to hand over the leadership of God's people. So he did. And he took the chance to speak his mind to the people. This could be painful for the Israelites.

👁 Read 1 Sam 12 v 1–5

ENGAGE YOUR BRAIN

▶ *What point was Samuel making? (v1–3)*

▶ *Why do you think he did this?*

▶ *Any hints here about how the new king should behave?*

Sadly, the rest of the Israelites hadn't behaved as well as Samuel.

👁 Read verses 6–13

▶ *How would you sum up how the people had acted?*

▶ *And what about God? (v7–8, v11)*

Although Israel turned their backs on God repeatedly, He didn't abandon them, or ignore their self-centred prayers (v10). In fact, He sent judges to rescue His ungrateful people (v11). And even when they rejected God as King, He was unbelievably patient and gave them a human king.

👁 Read verses 14–15

▶ *What choice did Saul and the Israelites now face?*

▶ *What were the consequences?*

God hadn't given up on His people yet. He gave them yet another chance. If they stopped rebelling, and served and obeyed Him, then they could expect the good life with God. But if they turned against God again, they could expect His punishment. And God makes the same offer to people today.

PRAY ABOUT IT

Admit your unfaithfulness to God. Thank Him for His faithfulness in sending Jesus to bring you rescue and forgiveness. Pray for people you know who still rebel against God, that they would recognise what Jesus has done for them.

→ TAKE IT FURTHER

More stuff on page 115.

39 | Rain of thought

Old man Samuel is giving the Israelites an earful for turning away from God and wanting their own king. And the Lord is going to do something spectacular to make them pay attention.

👁 Read 1 Sam 12 v 16–19

ENGAGE YOUR BRAIN

▶ *How did God convince His rebellious people they were in trouble? (v16–18)*

▶ *What did they beg Samuel to do?*

This thunderstorm was terrifying — it didn't usually rain at harvest time. The Israelites realised that God could easily destroy them and they deserved it. So they asked Samuel to talk to God on their behalf.

👁 Read verses 20-25

▶ *What must the people not do again? (v20–21)*

▶ *Why wouldn't God reject His people? (v22)*

▶ *What great advice did Samuel give them? (v24)*

▶ *What would happen if they ignored it? (v25)*

GET ON WITH IT

Which of these lessons do you must need to learn?

1. Don't let anything take God's place in your life (v21).

2. Cheer up! Even though we've let God down, He still loves His children (v22)! If you've had your sins forgiven by God, He will never leave you.

3. Serving God is more than going to church and reading your Bible. It means doing **everything** for Him. Yep, that includes work/school/college, relationships, playing sport, shopping, conversations. Everything. We must do all these things in a way that honours God.

PRAY ABOUT IT

So, which of these things do you need to talk about to God right now?

→ TAKE IT FURTHER

More of God's greatness on p115.

40 | Saul slips up

Samuel's warning was strong — God's king was to live God's way or the whole of Israel would suffer the consequences. Saul started off well, but how would he continue?

Read 1 Samuel 13 v 1–10

ENGAGE YOUR BRAIN

▷ What did Saul's son Jonathan do? (v3–4)

▷ How did the Philistines react? (v5)

▷ What effect did this have on the Israelites? (v6–7)

▷ What did Saul do when his patience and nerve ran out? (v8–10)

So, Jonathan attacked Israel's enemy. Saul took the credit. The Philistines gathered a massive army. The Israelites wet themselves in panic. Saul waited for God's messenger, Samuel. Samuel was late. Saul offered sacrifices to God without Samuel being there. So what?

Read verses 11–15

▷ What did Samuel say about Saul's actions? (v13)

▷ What was the tragic result? (v14)

Before a big battle, God's people would offer sacrifices to the Lord. It showed their trust in God and need for His help. But only the priest was allowed to do it. Saul ignored God's instructions. So God took away his family's right to rule Israel.

PRAY ABOUT IT

The Bible shows us how to live God's way. Think of a couple of ways you've disobeyed God recently. Say sorry to God. Ask His help with the areas you struggle in. Pray that even when life's hard, you'll obey His word.

THE BOTTOM LINE

Obey God or face the consequences.

→ TAKE IT FURTHER

Don't slip on your way to page 115.

51

41 | Daring raid

King Saul's up against the mighty Philistine army. Loads of Israelites are so terrified that they're either hiding or have run away. And things are about to get worse for Israel.

👁 Read 1 Samuel 13 v 16–23

ENGAGE YOUR BRAIN

▶ *What was the bad news for Israel's army?*

How could the tiny Israelite army fight the might of Philistine army with no weapons???

👁 Read 1 Sam 14 v 1–14

▶ *What did Jonathan decide to do?*

▶ *What was King Saul doing while Jonathan risked his life? (v2)*

▶ *What did Jonathan know about God? (v6)*

▶ *What did God help Jonathan to do? (v12–14)*

While his father sat under a tree being indecisive, Jonathan and his armour carrrier took on a daring raid by themselves. Despite having a priest with him, Saul didn't seek God's guidance. But Jonathan trusted that God was with him, giving him success against the odds. Unlike Saul, Jonathan showed his faith in God and the Lord gave him victory.

GET ON WITH IT

▶ *Is there a big decision you've been putting off?*

▶ *Is there something you need to do for God but you lack the courage to do it?*

▶ *How can you be more like Jonathan this week?*

PRAY ABOUT IT

We can't do great things for God by ourselves — we need God to help us. Thank the Lord that He's always there for His people. Maybe there's something you need to ask God's help with right now.

→ TAKE IT FURTHER

A little bit more on page 115.

42 ┊ Philistine phear ┊

With God's help, Jonathan and his armour bearer climbed a cliff face and killed loads of enemy Philistines. Let's check out the reactions of both the Philistines and King Saul.

👁 **Read 1 Sam 14 v 15–19**

ENGAGE YOUR BRAIN
▷ *What happened in the Philistine camp and who caused it? (v15)*

▷ *How was Saul hesitating? (v18–19)*

Their enemies are terrified and ready to be defeated. But instead of realising it was from God and acting quickly, Saul took a roll call and then got the priest to ask God what to do. He'd not sussed that God was already helping them!

THINK IT OVER
▷ *Do you recognise when God's at work in your life?*

▷ *Do you thank Him when He answers your prayers?*

👁 **Read verses 20-23**
▷ *What did Saul and his small army finally do? (v20)*

▷ *Who joined them? (v21–22)*

▷ *Who really won the battle? (v23)*

Despite Saul being hesitant, many Israelites being terrified and the Philistines having a mighty army, God rescued His people. They were weak, but God is strong. When we achieve things, we need to remember that we can do nothing great for God without His help. We should stop boasting and give Him the glory.

PRAY ABOUT IT
Thank the Lord that He does amazing things in our lives, even when we're useless. Give Him the praise He deserves for prayers that He has answered.

THE BOTTOM LINE
The Lord is behind our victories.

→ **TAKE IT FURTHER**
Earth-shaking stuff on page 116.

43 | Honey business

King Saul and the Israelite army have won a great victory over the Philistines. They must be exhausted and starving. Get ready for a strange tale involving foolish promises and honey-tipped swords.

👁 Read 1 Sam 14 v 24–35

ENGAGE YOUR BRAIN

▷ What did King Saul declare? (v24)

▷ Who disobeyed the king? (v27)

▷ What good point did Jonathan make? (v29–30)

▷ How did some of the soldiers break God's law? (v32–33)

👁 Read verses 36–46

▷ What did the priest have to persuade Saul to do? (v36)

▷ What was God's response to Saul's question? (v37)

▷ What did Saul realise this meant? (v38)

▷ What was his second rash promise of the day? (v39, v44)

▷ What was the great response of the soldiers? (v45)

Saul wasn't turning out to be the perfect king the people had wanted. He made rash, reckless promises to God (v24, 39); he clearly didn't offer sacrifices to God very often (v35); or ask for guidance (v36); and he was prepared to kill his own son, even though God had used Jonathan to rescue His people. God's people had asked for a king, but he would lead them into trouble because he didn't rule God's way.

THINK IT OVER

▷ Ever made quick, foolish promises to God?
▷ Ever failed to give God what He deserves?
▷ Do you ask God to help you make big decisions?

PRAY ABOUT IT

Talk these issues over with God, asking Him to help you become more and more useful to Him.

➔ TAKE IT FURTHER

More king kraziness on page 116.

44 ¦ Good king or bad king?

We've read a little about the kind of king Saul was. He didn't always obey God and yet he led Israel to many great military victories.

👁 Read 1 Sam 14 v 47–52

ENGAGE YOUR BRAIN

▶ How is Saul's military leadership summed up? (v47–48)

▶ What do we learn about Saul's family? (v49–51)

▶ Who was Israel's main enemy during King Saul's reign? (v52)

▶ How did Saul build up a strong royal guard? (v52)

Saul had a brilliant military record. Under his leadership, Israel defeated enemies in the north (Zobah), south (Edom), east (Moab, Ammonites) and west (Philistines). God used King Saul to rescue His people from their enemies.

But we've also seen that Saul didn't submit to God as his King. He did his own thing. So even though he was successful in battle, Saul wasn't successful in the most important way — living God's way. Tomorrow we'll read what God thought of Saul as king of His people.

THINK IT OVER

▶ Do other people think you're a "successful" Christian?

▶ Why/why not?

▶ But what's the truth on the inside — are you really living for God?

▶ In which specific ways do you need to submit to God as King, and live His way?

PRAY ABOUT IT

Thanks God that He's King of your life. Pray that you will let Him rule in every part of your life.

THE BOTTOM LINE

Who's King of your life?

→ TAKE IT FURTHER

No *Take it further* today.

Destruction instruction

Are you any good at following instructions for building something or setting up electrical equipment? They're casually straightforward, but if you ignore them you could end up in a mess.

Over the last few days, we've seen how King Saul was useless at following God's instructions. Now God has another task for Saul and the Israelites.

👁 Read 1 Sam 15 v 1–11

▷ *Why should Saul listen to Samuel? (v1)*

▷ *What was God's specific instruction to Saul? (v3)*

▷ *Why?*

▷ *How did Saul rightly treat the Kenite tribe? (v6)*

▷ *How did he fail to follow God's instructions? (v9)*

▷ *How did God feel about this? (v11)*

The Amalekites had attacked God's people, so God rightly told Saul to wipe them out. They'd gone against God so they deserved it. Yet again,

Saul failed to fully follow God's orders. God was grieved that His chosen king refused to obey Him.

Sin is when we choose our own way instead of God's. When we think we know better than God. When we refuse to obey Him. And it upsets Him to be treated like this.

GET ON WITH IT

▷ *Which of God's instructions are you refusing to follow?*

▷ *What will you do about it right now?*

PRAY ABOUT IT

Say sorry to God and plead for His help.

THE BOTTOM LINE

Follow God fully.

→ TAKE IT FURTHER

Follow these instructions: Go to page 167. Engage your brain. Learn more about God and His methods.

46 ┆ Royal rejection ┆

Things are not looking good for King Saul. Yet again he failed to obey God's instructions. Samuel is now on his way to see Saul and it won't be a happy meeting.

👁 Read 1 Sam 15 v 12–19

ENGAGE YOUR BRAIN

▶ What selfish mistake did Saul make? (v12)

▶ And what crazy claim did he make? (v13)

▶ What was Sam's problem with Saul? (19)

Saul was now taking the glory himself instead of giving it to God (v12). He even tried to cover up his disobedience with lies and excuses. To God's prophet, Samuel. Big mistake.

👁 Read verses 20–23

▶ What did Saul continue to claim? (v20–21)

▶ What was more important to God than sacrifices? (v22)

▶ What had Saul done? (v23)

▶ So what would God do to him?

No amount of sacrifices could make up for Saul's disobedience. By continually ignoring God's commands, he was rejecting God — the most serious crime of all. So God would reject Saul and raise up a new king over Israel.

We won't please God by just appearing to serve Him. It may fool people around us, but it won't fool God. What really pleases Him is obedience. Living our lives for Him. Obeying what we read in the Bible.

PRAY ABOUT IT

Ask God to help you be obedient to Him. Mention specific areas where you struggle to obey the Lord.

THE BOTTOM LINE

Obey God fully.

→ TAKE IT FURTHER

Don't be a reject — turn to page 116.

47 That's torn it

Ever messed up really badly and offended someone? You'll do anything to make things right and not lose them. King Saul was feeling like that, but sometimes it's sadly too late.

👁 Read 1 Sam 15 v 24–35

ENGAGE YOUR BRAIN

▶ What did Saul admit? (v24)

▶ What did he ask for? (v25)

▶ What terrible news did Samuel hit Saul with? (v26)

▶ What was the sad truth for disobedient Saul? (v28)

▶ What did Samuel remind Saul about God? (v29)

In the next issue of Engage, we'll read how God chose David to be king of Israel in place of Saul.

👁 Read verses 30–35

▶ What did Saul ask Sam again? (v30)

▶ What did Samuel do? (v31–33)

▶ And then what? (v34–35)

▶ How did God feel about the whole sad situation? (v35)

Saul continued to disobey and reject the Lord. God had given Saul so many chances, but eventually He rejected Saul as king. It upset God and His prophet Samuel that this had to happen, but sin can't be ignored.

GET ON WITH IT

▶ What do you do that upsets God?

▶ What do you need to do about it?

PRAY ABOUT IT

It's time to bring these things before God.

→ TAKE IT FURTHER

Ripping stuff on page 116.

Paul on tour

In 2005, the Rolling Stones embarked on a 147-date, two-year world tour. At one gig, on Rio de Janeiro beach in Brazil, they played to 2 million people. By the end of the "A bigger bang" tour, they had made £370 million.

That made it the highest grossing tour ever; but not the highest impact. That title must belong to the apostle Paul, whose tours took him from Israel through modern-day Turkey and Greece, and eventually all the way to Rome. And at each gig, Paul had a simple message for the thousands who listened: Jesus died for sins,

Jesus has risen in glory, Jesus offers you eternal life.

Critical reaction to Paul's performances was mixed. Many sneered; lots rioted; and some accepted Jesus as Lord of their lives, and with Paul's help set up churches. Two thousand years later we can still learn a lot from these early Christians about how faith in Jesus shapes life, what good churches and pastors look like, and how God works in and through His people.

So dive into Acts 16 – 20, jump back to AD49-57, and join Paul on tour!

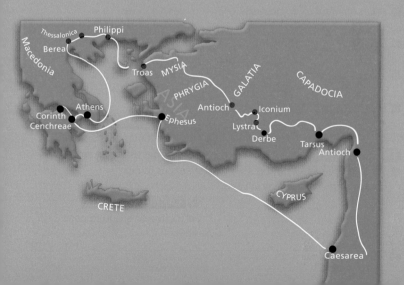

48 | Follow the diversion

Ever been on a car journey and found out the route won't work — there's a big "DIVERSION" sign saying you have to go a different way? Life can be like that, too. Our plans can get seriously diverted.

👁 Read Acts 16 v 1–5

Poor Timothy. He got circumcised (ouch!) to respect Jewish tradition so they could both gain entry to Jewish synogogues as they travelled to preach the gospel. Notice how well it all seems to be going (v5).

👁 Read verses 6–10

ENGAGE YOUR BRAIN

▶ What was Paul's plan and who put up a diversion sign? (v6)

▶ What did Paul try to do next? (v7)

▶ Did it work? Why/why not? (v7)

▶ What happened next? (v9)

▶ How did Paul and his companions react? Why? (v10)

THINK IT OVER

▶ Why had the Spirit put up a couple of diversion signs in v6–8?

As we'll see, Paul's time in Macedonia proved to be a great success for the gospel. Lots of churches were set up, and loads of people became Christians. Being diverted there was a great idea of God's!

▶ What does this section show about how God works in people's lives?

PRAY ABOUT IT

Ask the Spirit to guide and change your plans, and to help you trust Him as He directs your life.

THE BOTTOM LINE

God sometimes puts up diversion signs to get us to just where He wants us to be.

➔ TAKE IT FURTHER

Follow the diversion to page 117.

49 ¦ My job, God's job

In (American) football, different players have different jobs. Some are purely blockers; others are runners; one guy is the quarterback. When they all do their job, the results are great! Evangelism's a bit like that...

👁 Read Acts 16 v 11–14

ENGAGE YOUR BRAIN

▶ Where do Paul and his group get to? (v12)

▶ Where do they go to speak to people about Jesus? (v13)

▶ What happens to Lydia? (v14)

THINK IT THROUGH

▶ Who told Lydia about Jesus?

▶ Who converted Lydia to being a follower of Jesus? (end of v14)

▶ When it comes to people becoming Christians, what is our part in it?

▶ What is God's role?

▶ How is this encouraging for us (especially if we find it hard)?

PRAY ABOUT IT

▶ What should we be asking God to help us to do, and what should we be asking God to do?

Pray in that way for some of the people you know well who aren't yet Christians.

👁 Read verse 15

Here we see two signs of someone who's truly become a "believer in the Lord." Lydia is baptised, to show she's a member of God's family; and she invites Paul and his friends to stay at her house, showing she wants to look out for God's family.

THE BOTTOM LINE

God works in people's hearts as His people tell them about His Son.

→ TAKE IT FURTHER

Just the job — page 117.

50 | Points of view

Today, you're going to walk in the shoes of the people we meet.

THE SLAVE GIRL

👁 Read Acts 16 v 16–24

▶ What was your problem? (v16)
▶ What did you know about Paul and Silas? (v17)
▶ What happened, and why? (v18)
▶ Why is knowing Jesus good news for you?

THE JAILER

👁 Read verses 25–34

▶ What was your problem? (v25-27)

If your prisoners escape, you get executed. So you're face to face with your own death. But Paul and the other prisoners haven't run away…

▶ What do you want to know? (v30)

You've come close to dying — and you don't like it. You know these guys are telling people "the way to be saved", but what is it? What do you need to be saved from eternal death?

▶ What does Paul tell you? (v31)
▶ How do you react? (v33–34)
▶ Why is knowing Jesus good news for you?

Knowing Jesus brings release from the power of evil; and release from the fear of death.

PAUL AND SILAS

▶ What happened to you? (v22–24)
▶ How did you react? (v25)

After all they'd been through, Paul and Silas were still praising God and looking to tell others about His Son! They didn't see prison as a problem; they saw it as a possibility to tell more people the good news.

THINK IT THROUGH

▶ How does Paul and Silas' example encourage and challenge you today?

➔ TAKE IT FURTHER

Another point of view on page 117.

51 | Be a Berean

Ever heard of the Bereans? No? Well, it's time to see what they were like; because all Christians should aim to be a Berean.

👁 Read Acts 17 v 1–9

ENGAGE YOUR BRAIN
▶ *Where does Paul get to? (v1)*

▶ *What does Paul get on with doing? (v2)*

▶ *What's his main message? (v3)*

▶ *What effects does his Bible teaching have? (v4–5)*

So Paul moves on to Berea (v10)

👁 Read verses 10–15

▶ *What makes the Bereans of "noble character"? (v11)*

▶ *When Paul said something, what did they do? (v11)*

▶ *What effects did Paul's Bible teaching have here? (v12)*

It didn't last. Though the Bereans were up for Paul's Bible teaching, many Thessalonians weren't; look what they did in v13–15.

THINK IT THROUGH
▶ *When people examine the Bible, what do they see about Jesus? (v2–3)*

▶ *How can we check whether what a preacher says is true? (v11)*

GET ON WITH IT
▶ *What can you learn from the Bereans?*

▶ *What can you change to be a better "Berean"?*

THE BOTTOM LINE
Be a Berean.

→ TAKE IT FURTHER
More stuff on page 117.

52 | Idol capital

What upsets you most in life?
What gets you really worked up?
What do you do to stop it upsetting you?

👁 Read Acts 17 v 16

ENGAGE YOUR BRAIN
▶ *Where had Paul reached now? (v16)*

▶ *How was Paul feeling? (v16)*

▶ *What made Paul feel like that? (v16)*

This was the Roman Empire's capital of ideas. Its people loved to think and talk about religion, and God, and life and death (v21). An idol is something which people treat as God instead of Him. And Athens was the capital of idols. In those days, idols were often statues; today we may not treat statues as God but we still have idols; money, popularity, sex, career, family, anything that we love and serve and respect as our "god", as the thing which is most important to us.

▶ *Why do you think these idols made Paul feel this way?*

▶ *How much respect was the one true God getting in this city?*

If we love God, we'll hate seeing others refusing to even recognise His existence.

👁 Read verses 17–21

▶ *What did Paul do? (v17)*

▶ *What was his basic message? (end v18)*

THINK ABOUT IT
▶ *How distressed are you when people around you treat something else as their god and ignore Jesus?*

▶ *Does this prompt you to talk to them about Jesus' resurrection?*

THE BOTTOM LINE
Idols should distress us; distress should prompt us to talk about Jesus.

→ TAKE IT FURTHER
More idol talk on page 118.

53 | Knowing and needing

Who is God? What is He like?
The Athenians knew that they didn't know.
And Paul knew that he did know.
Let's listen in and learn.

👁 Read Acts 17 v 22–28
The Athenians accepted that they didn't really know who God was (v23). So Paul said he'd explain God to them.

ENGAGE YOUR BRAIN
▷ *Why should this be good news to the Athenians?*

▷ *From v24–26, fill in the list:*

God doesn't…

God has…

▷ *What should be people's response to this God? (v27)*

THINK IT THROUGH
▷ *Does God need anything from you? Why/why not?*

▷ *Do you need God? Why/why not?*

If God needed us to do stuff for Him, then He'd owe us; we'd be able to be in charge of Him and His actions. But as we need God to do stuff for us, then we owe Him; He's in charge of us and should direct our actions. The Athenians needed to realise that it wasn't for them to say what God is like; it's for God to reveal what He's like.

How do you think the Athenians will react to what Paul's told them? (remember that Athens is full of temples). We'll find out tomorrow.

PRAY ABOUT IT
God, thank you for all that you've done for me and continue to do for me. Help me to remember that I need you, and you don't need me. Make my life revolve around you, and stop me from thinking that you should revolve around me. Amen.

→ TAKE IT FURTHER
More knowledge on page 118.

54 | A day in God's diary

If someone said: "What does Jesus rising from the dead mean?", what would you say? Paul gives a clear — and surprising — answer to that question as he tells the Athenians about the God who can be known.

Read Acts 17 v 29–34

ENGAGE YOUR BRAIN

▷ Who are humans created by? (v29)

▷ How's Paul pointing out the stupidity of worshipping an idol (something made by man)?

▷ What does God now tell all people to do? (v30)

Repent means to turn around. All people everywhere have worshipped an idol — something that becomes more important to them than God. They need to start treating their Creator as their God.

▷ Because of humanity's idolatry, what kind of day has God put in his diary? (v31)

▷ Who'll do the judging? How do we know that? (v31)

▷ What does Jesus rising from the dead prove? (v31)

THINK IT THROUGH

The only way to escape Jesus' judgment of idolatry in the future is to turn away from idols and towards Jesus as God right now.

▷ Have you ever done that?

▷ In which areas of your life do you struggle to love and serve and obey Jesus as God, instead of something else?

SHARE IT

▷ Think of some friends you'd love to tell about Jesus. What are they treating as God instead of Him?

▷ How can you tell them that Jesus is better than those things, and that judgment is coming?

→ TAKE IT FURTHER

Verses 32–34 are covered on p118.

55 | Me? A minister?

Who do you know who's a minister?
Actually; what is a minister? That's easy —
it's someone who works for a church... isn't it?

👁 **Read Acts 18 v 1–4**

ENGAGE YOUR BRAIN

▶ *Where's next on Paul's tour?*

▶ *Paul went to stay with a couple of friends (v2). What did he do with them? (v3)*

▶ *So, what was Paul doing from Monday to Friday?*

▶ *What did Paul do at the weekends?*

THINK IT THROUGH

▶ *What was Paul's ministry?*

▶ *Was it his full-time job?*

▶ *What does this show us about who can do ministry?*

▶ *Is having a full-time job an excuse for not having a ministry?*

God calls members of His people to different ministries. Some have a preaching ministry; others are evangelists (like Paul here); some teach children the Bible; others meet with individual Christians to encourage them.

It's easy to think that only "proper" ministers who work full-time for a church will be asked by God to do these things; but Paul's example shows us that a full-time job and ministry can go hand-in-hand.

GET ON WITH IT

▶ *What ministry do you think God might want you to help?*

▶ *Are there times when you're not working (at school, college, uni or job) when you won't take time for yourself but instead use it to serve God's people?*

➔ **TAKE IT FURTHER**
Weird Corinth facts on page 118.

56 | Paul's panic

It's so easy to think that Paul just breezed into a city, talked about Jesus, and everyone thought he was great and became Christians. But it wasn't quite like that...

👁 Read Acts 18 v 5–6

ENGAGE YOUR BRAIN

▷ Who did Paul preach to about the Christ, God's eternal king? (v5)

Sensible idea: they were God's ancient people, and knew their Old Testaments. They'll be thrilled to hear that Christ has come into the world!

▷ How did it go? (v6)

Ever been attacked for being a Christian? You've got something in common with Paul.

👁 Read v7–8

▷ How did Paul react? (v7)

Strange result: God's ancient people don't want to know about Jesus, so Paul's going to preach to outsiders.

▷ How did it go? (v8)

👁 Read v9–17

▷ How was Paul feeling about talking about Jesus in Corinth? (v9)

▷ But he didn't need to feel like this — why not? (v10)

Stunning truth: Jesus has chosen lots of people in Corinth to be His followers; and He's going to use Paul to reach them.

THINK ABOUT IT

▷ Are Jesus' people always the ones we'd expect to become Christians? (Think about v5–8.)

▷ How does Jesus reach His people to make them Christians? (Think about v10–11.)

▷ How is this an encouragement to you as a Christian?

THE BOTTOM LINE

Jesus uses His people to reach more of His people; and often His people are surprising people.

→ TAKE IT FURTHER

Don't panic! Go to page 119.

57 | Apeing Apollos

Acts 17 encouraged us to "be a Berean";
Acts 18 wants us to "ape Apollos", to learn
from and follow his example.

👁 Read Acts 18 v 18–23

ENGAGE YOUR BRAIN

Paul's time in Corinth has finished and
he's moved on. Meanwhile…

👁 Read v24–28

▶ *Who do we meet in v24, and
how's he described? (v24–25)*

"He knew only the baptism of John."
In other words, he knew that John
the Baptist had said Jesus was God's
promised King. But there were some
important gaps in his understanding.
He knew that he needed to repent —
turn from sin and back to God. But he
didn't fully understand about Jesus'
death and resurrection.

▶ *When they hear him speak, what
do Paul's friends Priscilla and
Aquila do? (v26)*

▶ *Apollos clearly listened to them,
and decided to go to another
town to serve God there. What
did he do? (v27–28)*

THINK IT THROUGH

God gives us with these little pictures
of churches and Christians for us to
hold up alongside ourselves and ask
how we might live for God better
— both as individuals and churches.
Here, God wants us to "ape Apollos".

▶ *What can we learn from Apollos:
– when it comes to the Bible?
(v24, 28)
– when it comes to talking about
Jesus? (v25, 28)
– when it comes to being shown
a mistake? (v26)*

▶ *In which of these three areas will
you try to ape Apollos?*

THE BOTTOM LINE

Ape Apollos.

→ TAKE IT FURTHER

More monkey business on page 119.

How to interpret the Bible

One of the main ambitions of **engage** is to encourage you to dive into God's word and learn how to handle it and understand it more. Each issue, TOOLBOX gives you tips, tools and advice for wrestling with the Bible. This issue, how do we understand what the Bible is saying?

WHAT'S IT ALL ABOUT?

It's great to read the Bible, yet some parts of it can seem weird, boring or impossible to understand. But there are tools we can use to interpret the Bible. When you interpret something, you make it clear and understandable.

But it's not just about understanding what a passage in the Bible is saying, it's also about applying that meaning to your life. The question isn't just what is the Bible teaching, but what is it teaching *me*, and what should I do about it? As James says: *"Do not merely listen to the word, and so deceive yourselves. Do what it says."* (James 1 v 22)

The Bible teacher R.C. Sproul came up with three principles for understanding God's word.

1. INTERPRET THE BIBLE BY THE BIBLE

If a passage is hard to understand, it's often much clearer in another part of the Bible. This is where a cross-reference Bible comes in handy — it lists other parts of the Bible that are related to the verse you're looking at. And if you're still unsure where to look, ask an older Christian.

The *context* of a Bible bit is also vital. If you're unsure about a verse, read what comes before it and after it. What are those verses saying? Just as it's tempting to believe a rumour about someone even if it's totally out of character, it's tempting to take something in the Bible out of context. In both cases, all it does is make you feel better, even if you're wrong. When it comes to people, consider their character; when it comes to the Bible, consider the context.

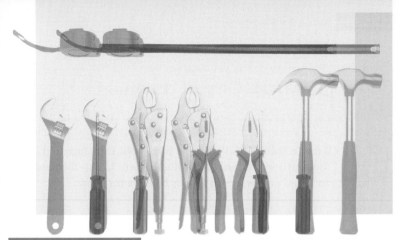

2. INTERPRET WHAT IS THERE

We should interpret the Bible *as it is written*. Don't read something into it that isn't there, and don't skip over something that is. Because the Bible speaks honestly about humans and our relationships with God and with each other, we sometimes get offended by what we read in the Bible. Don't add to or take away from what's there on the page (Deuteronomy 12 v 32).

3. INTERPRET THE BIBLE OBJECTIVELY

It's easy to interpret the Bible subjectively — according to your own viewpoints and desires. This can lead to serious disagreements, both with the Bible and with each other. As you read the Bible, focus on what it says rather than what you already believe. One Bible boffin wrote:
"One must first ask what a Scripture was intended to mean to the people for whom it was originally written. Only then is the interpreter free to ask what meaning it has for Christians today."

Avoid the temptation to stamp your own impressions or feelings on what you read before you discover the objective truth it contains. This doesn't mean you shouldn't come to your own conclusions about what the Bible means, but your own interpretation should be guided by the context, what the rest of the Bible teaches and what the aim of the author was at the time. The Bible is the word of God, it comes straight from Him, so we can trust God's word to mean what it says.

LIVE BY WHAT YOU LEARN

Once you learn how to interpret the Bible, you can become someone who *"correctly explains the word of truth"* (2 Timothy 2 v 15). That means we're not to keep it to ourselves. It's not about understanding the Bible and just growing in knowledge. We have to make sure we apply what we learn to the way we live. And also share it with others. God's word is for everyone — read it, understand it, apply it, spread it!

58 ISAIAH: City of dreams

Back to Isaiah. God's people have split into Judah in the south and Israel in the north. Here Isaiah focuses on Israel and what God's got in store for them.

👁 Read Isaiah 9 v 8–17

ENGAGE YOUR BRAIN

▶ *What did they think they could do after God punished them? (v10)*

▶ *What did this show about them? (v9)*

▶ *But what would God do? (v11–12)*

▶ *Why?*

▶ *What else would result? (v14–16)*

👁 Read Isaiah 9 v 18 – 10 v 4

▶ *Who specifically would be punished? (10 v 1–2)*

▶ *What is repeated four times? (9 v 12, 17, 21, 10 v 4)*

▶ *What is the terrifying news for those who reject God?*

Isaiah's not exactly a laugh-a-minute, is he? But neither is the truth for

those who go against God. The sad truth is judgment *is* terrifying. There will be nowhere to hide when Jesus returns as Judge. God's enemies will be handed over to a life without His love and mercy. No one can escape God's punishment unless they trust Jesus to rescue them.

PRAY ABOUT IT

Sorry to start this section of Isaiah on such a downer. But that's how serious sin is. And that's why it's urgent that we pray for our unbelieving friends — that God will have mercy on them and rescue them.

THE BOTTOM LINE

God's judgment is terrifying.

→ TAKE IT FURTHER

A bit more on page 119.

59 | Axe of justice

It often seems that evil people are out of control. They seem to get away with it. But Isaiah shows us that God can use even the actions of evil men to achieve His purposes.

👁 Read Isaiah 10 v 5–19

ENGAGE YOUR BRAIN

▶ *How did God use Assyria? (v5–6)*

▶ *But what would happen to Assyria? (v15–19)*

▶ *Why? (v12–14)*

This all happened. In 722BC, Assyria completely wiped out the nation of Israel. They then attacked God's people in Judah, but Judah survived. The Assyrians were not serving God, they were selfishly trying to conquer the world. Yet God used them to punish His rebellious people. And then He punished Assyria for *their* rejection of Him.

👁 Read verses 20–34

▶ *What different names refer to God? (v20, v21, v24)*

▶ *What did God promise? (v20–22)*

▶ *And what would God do to His people's enemies? (v25)*

In v15, Assyria was an axe destroying nations. It thought it was safe from God's judgment. But v33–34 tells us that God would wield the axe against Assyria, destroying them for their rejection of Him.

In many parts of Isaiah there are both darkness and light. Here the darkness is the crippling punishment of Israel and Assyria. The light is hope beyond this punishment for a trusting remnant, through a perfect King. (More on this tomorrow.)

PRAY ABOUT IT

Thank God that powerful nations and terrorists don't have the last word in human history. It's God who's in control. Ask God to help you be humble and repentant and trusting in Jesus for forgiveness.

➔ TAKE IT FURTHER

Axe facts on page 119.

73

60 | Branching out

Ready for more misery from Isaiah? Hope not, because today Isaiah is bursting with great news for God's people. Really, he is!

👁 Read Isaiah 11 v 1–9

ENGAGE YOUR BRAIN

▷ *What would be the character of this special person? (v2–3)*

▷ *How will He rule? (v3–5)*

▷ *What will the world be like with Him as King? (v6–9)*

Jesse was the father of King David, Israel's greatest king. *"A shoot ... from the stump of Jesse"* is the new King David. No prizes for guessing this is talking about Jesus Christ. When He returns as King, His reign will be awesome. He will rule with perfect justice and the whole of creation will be affected by His reign. There will be perfect peace.

👁 Read verses 10–16

▷ *What will this King do on "that day"? (v10–16)*

God's new King will gather His scattered people from all ends of the earth. What an incredible picture of the future for God's people. And the future has already begun.

Jesus already rules over His church — Christians everywhere. But His reign isn't total yet. One day, Jesus will return to rule over all creation. His people will live with Him in perfection.

PRAY ABOUT IT

Take your time to read through chapter 11 again, turning it into a prayer of praise to King Jesus.

THE BOTTOM LINE

Jesus rules.

➡ TAKE IT FURTHER

Take the branch line to page 119.

61 | Sing your hearts out

Ever wondered how best to worship God and what worship really involves? Well, today Isaiah gives us a crash course in true worship.

👁 Read Isaiah 12 v 1–3

ENGAGE YOUR BRAIN

▷ *Find at least four things to praise God for in these verses.*

-
-
-
-

▷ *How had God turned things around for His people?*

Isaiah has been telling God's people how the Lord would punsh them, but here He says God's anger will be turned away. Jesus' death and resurrection makes it possible for people to be forgiven and for God's anger to be turned away. He will rescue them, giving them the strength they need. His song will be on their hearts and they will be no longer be afraid. This is what we should praise and worship God for.

👁 Read verses 4–6

▷ *What should be our response to what God has done for us? (v5–6)*

▷ *Who should we tell about God? (v4)*

Through Jesus, God has rescued His people. Their hideous sins have been forgiven. They will go to live with Him in perfection for ever. This should lead to us singing and praising God all the time! And we should want to share the news with everyone. And live in a way that pleases our Saviour. That's what worship is.

THINK IT OVER

▷ *How do you need to change the way you worship God?*

PRAY ABOUT IT

Read this chapter over, stopping at each verse to use it as a starting point for your prayers.

THE BOTTOM LINE

Sing to the Lord for He has done glorious things.

➔ TAKE IT FURTHER

Find a different tune on page 120.

62 | Bad bad Babylon

Today we enter a whole new section of Isaiah. Chapters 13–27 look forward to a coming day. God rules the nations and shows it in acts of judgment that point us ahead to God's world-shaking final day.

👁 Read Isaiah 13 v 1–22

ENGAGE YOUR BRAIN

▷ Babylon would defeat God's people, but what would God do to Babylon? (v5–6)

▷ Why? (v11)

▷ Who would God use to do this? (v17)

Isaiah is pointing us to two big events at once. Clever. He talks about God's judgment on Babylon (this happened in 539 BC). But it's also looking forward to the final day when God will punish everyone who has rejected Him. Check out v9–13 to see how terrifying it will be for the godless.

👁 Read Isaiah 14 v 1–23

▷ What words of hope were there for God's people? (v1–2)

▷ What had Babylon thought would happen? (v13–14)

▷ How did God deal with their arrogance? (v15–17, v22–23)

The defeat of God's enemies would be the victory of God's people. God's people could take heart. God would act against evil and punish it. And beyond that judgment, He'd rescue and restore those who trusted Him. One coming day, He'll do that finally and ultimately.

PRAY ABOUT IT

Thank God that evil won't be allowed to succeed for ever. Thank Him for setting aside a day when He will bring final, perfect justice.

→ TAKE IT FURTHER

Why Babylon? Turn to page 120.

63 | God's enemies defeated

Yesterday we heard God's bad news for evil Babylon. More enemies of God's people are now in the firing line — this time it's Assyria (again), the Philistines, and Moab.

👁 Read Isaiah 14 v 24–32

ENGAGE YOUR BRAIN

▷ *What happens when God plans something? (v24, v26–27)*

▷ *What did this mean for Assyria? (v25)*

▷ *And for the Philistines? (v30)*

▷ *What was the news for God's people in Zion (Jerusalem)? (v32)*

God's perfect plans for the world cannot be stopped.

👁 Read Isaiah 16 v 1–14

▷ *How does v5 look forward to Jesus?*

▷ *What did God think of Moab's boasting? (v6)*

▷ *So what would happen to Moab? (v13–14)*

King David once ruled over Moab. Now Moabite refugees were again seeking refuge from David's family. Isaiah points to a day when people from all nations will look to Jesus, the Son of David, to protect them and provide justice.

PRAY ABOUT IT

Pray that your family and friends will turn to find refuge in Jesus from the judgment of God.

→ TAKE IT FURTHER

Find the missing chapter on page 120.

64 | Dread zone

Isaiah is delivering dread from God to the nations that oppose Him and His people. Next up is Damascus, capital of Syria (Aram). As always in God's word, there's a message for us too.

👁 Read Isaiah 17 v 1–6

ENGAGE YOUR BRAIN

▶ *What would happen to Damascus? (v1)*

▶ *Where else would be destroyed with them? (v2–3)*

▶ *Yet what hope was there? (v6)*

Aroer and Ephraim were parts of Israel, the northern kingdom. Israel would go down when God slammed Damascus. Israel would be punished for seeking an alliance with Syria and relying on Syria instead of God.

👁 Read verses 7–14

▶ *Who will people turn to? (v7)*

▶ *And turn away from? (v8)*

▶ *Why would these places be destroyed? (v10)*

▶ *What would happen to all God's enemies? (v13)*

God's judgment may seem harsh, yet it comes from His great love for people. He punishes people to show how wrongly they've acted, in the hope that some will repent and turn back to Him (v7). There is still hope for those who turn to God.

PRAY ABOUT IT

Pray for friends who don't see a need for Jesus in their lives. Pray that they will see the seriousness of their situation, so they're driven to turn back to God.

THE BOTTOM LINE

There is hope in God's judgment.

➡ TAKE IT FURTHER

Grab more on page 120.

65 Walk like an Egyptian

Through Isaiah, God was announcing a day of judgment on all the nations around Judah — to the north, west, east... and now south. It showed God's people that they couldn't rely on other nations, they could only trust God.

👁 **Read Isaiah 18 v 1–7**

ENGAGE YOUR BRAIN

▷ *How were the people of Cush (Ethiopia) described? (v2)*

▷ *How would God show His disapproval for this aggressive nation? (v4–6)*

▷ *How would they respond? (v7)*

👁 **Speed read Isaiah 19 v 1–15**

▷ *What was God's message to Egypt? (v1–4)*

▷ *Why? (v3)*

Relying on your own resources and achievements? Trying to resolve problems without looking to God? That was Egypt. Now get ready for a twist in the tail...

👁 **Read verses 16–25**

▷ *What will happen "in that day"? (v16, v18, v19, v23, v24)*

▷ *What would be the amazing turn around for evil Egypt? (v25)*

Incredible. God would bring these people from fear (v16–17) to trust (v18) to wholehearted dedication to Him (v19–22). And what's this — Egypt and Assyria at peace? Surely not! Isaiah's pointing to a coming day when God would bring about reconciliation (with Himself and between nations). These transformed outsiders would become part of His people.

PRAY ABOUT IT

Thank God that in heaven people from every tribe, nation and language will sing the praises of Jesus. Ask Him to help you live your life in the light of this amazing promise.

⟶ **TAKE IT FURTHER**

Isaiah gets naked on page 120.

66 Valley of Vision

Who's in God's firing line this time? Babylon again, Edom, Arabia and, er, Jerusalem. Hold on, wasn't Jerusalem God's city, where His people lived?

👁 Read Isaiah 21 v 1–17

ENGAGE YOUR BRAIN

▶ What would happen to godless Babylon? (v9)

▶ And what about Arabia (Kedar)? (v16–17)

God's people in Judah turned to these nations for help, but these godless nations would have their power taken away from them by God. Judah put their trust in the wrong places.

👁 Read Isaiah 22 v 1–14

▶ What about Jerusalem's future drove Isaiah to tears? (v2–5)

▶ What response did God expect of His people? (v12)

▶ Yet what did He see? (v13)

▶ What was His verdict? (v14)

The unforgivable sin was unbelief — a refusal to turn to the Lord and repent (v12). Complete self-reliance.

👁 Read verses 15–25

Isaiah condemned Shebna, one of Jerusalem's officials. His authority would be given to Eliakim — if he stayed faithful. Verse 22 is quoted in Revelation 3 v 7. Eliakim points us to Jesus — God's most faithful servant — who is given the authority to let people into the new Jerusalem, God's eternal city.

PRAY ABOUT IT

Thank God for giving you a hope and a future that doesn't rely on world powers or other people's strength, but trusts in God and His eternal kingdom, set up by His Son Jesus.

→ TAKE IT FURTHER

More eating and drinking on p120.

67 | Flat Tyre

Tyre was an impressive port in the Mediterranean Sea. It was well-known for being wealthy, and people travelled from miles away to meet and trade there. But the people of Tyre had no time for God.

👁 Read Isaiah 23 v 1–8

ENGAGE YOUR BRAIN

▷ *How is Tyre described at the end of v3?*

▷ *Where did people travel from to trade in this great city? (v1–5)*

▷ *What would happen to Tyre? (v1)*

▷ *What do you think is the answer to the question in v8?*

👁 Read verses 9–14

▷ *What's the answer and why? (v9)*

▷ *How was Babylon a warning to these people? (v13)*

The Lord promised to destroy the proud city of Tyre, just as He wiped out evil Babylon. These people proudly relied on their own wealth rather than trusting in God. So He would punish them. (Tyre was eventually destroyed by Alexander the Great in 332BC.)

👁 Read verses 15–18

▷ *What would happen to Tyre after 70 years of anonymity? (v17)*

▷ *What amazing thing would happen with Tyre's wealth? (v18)*

Tyre would once again trade with other nations, but its earnings would go to God and His people. This happened when Tyre provided materials for rebuilding God's temple in Jerusalem (Ezra 3 v 7). But Isaiah also points us further into the future when nations' wealth will no longer be used for selfish purposes, but for God's glory and for His people.

Money and possessions are not to be used for our own selfish purposes or to fuel pride and popularity. It's all given to us by God, so we should use it to serve Him.

PRAY ABOUT IT

Ask God to change your view of money, so you use it for His glory. Talk to Him about ways you can do this.

➔ TAKE IT FURTHER

More about wealth and poverty on page 121.

68 | Devastation day

Since chapter 13, God's been naming and shaming nations who'd face His judgment, while hinting at a greater future for a remnant of His people. Next, no names as Isaiah tells us about God's final, coming, judgment day.

👁 Read Isaiah 24 v 1–13

ENGAGE YOUR BRAIN

▶ What's the devastating news? (v1)

▶ Who will this affect? (v2)

▶ Why will God punish the whole earth? (v5–6)

▶ Can you find a tiny glimmer of hope hidden at the ends of verses 6 and 13?

👁 Read verses 14–23

▶ How will the remnant — God's faithful people — react on this day of judgment? (v14–15)

▶ Yet what does Isaiah remind everone who turns away from God? (v17–18)

▶ What will happen on Judgment Day? (v19–23)

Terrible prospect: God executing His judgment (v21–22).

Glorious prospect: the Lord ruling His restored people. And with such a brightness that the sun and moon blush at how feeble they are in comparison (v23).

PRAY ABOUT IT

Thank God that His terrifying day of judgment is not bad news for believers. Thank Him that His punishment of Jesus on the cross has taken away our guilt. Use verses 14–16 to sing God's praises.

PRAY AGAIN

Let's not forget the horror of God's day of judgment. List at least 5 people who refuse to trust in Jesus:

-
-
-
-
-

Plead with God that He would rescue them from the road to destruction.

→ TAKE IT FURTHER

More fascinating stuff on page 121.

Forever faithful

Today, slow down. Avoid the "charge-through-this-I'm-in-a-hurry" routine. Chapter 25 contains truths that are worth exploring deeply. Remember, Isaiah's focus is still God's coming Judgment Day.

👁 Read Isaiah 25 v 1–5

ENGAGE YOUR BRAIN

- ▶ *Why does Isaiah sing God's praises? (v1)*
- ▶ *What surprising thing does he praise God for? (v2)*
- ▶ *What else? (v4–5)*
- ▶ *What will God's enemies do evenutally? (v3)*

So much to praise and thank God for: His faultless faithfulness; the incredible things He's done; His perfect plans; His fair punishment of those who oppose Him; the protection of His people. Don't you want to sing to God right now?

👁 Read verses 6–12

- ▶ *What does God promise?*
  v6:
  v7:
  v8a:
  v8b:
  v8c:
- ▶ *So what will eternal life with God be like?*

- ▶ *What will all God's people say? (v9)*
- ▶ *But what about proud people who rely on their own abilities? (v10–12)*

What covers the nations (v7) — sin and death ruling — will be gone. Forever. People from all nations will be in God's family (v6), and God will care for us personally (v8). Awesome.

Would you prefer a mountain rescue or a manure bath? (v10–11). Take your pick. But it's no joke, repentance and trust in God gets you to the heavenly feast. Pride, like Moab's, will keep you away, and bring you unimaginably terrible judgment.

PRAY ABOUT IT

Go through v1–8, one verse at a time, using them to shape your prayers of praise to God.

→ TAKE IT FURTHER

Revealing stuff on page 121.

Kelly Clark – Snowboarder

THE GIRL WITH EVERYTHING

When I was 18, I found myself in a place where I had accomplished everything that was in my heart to do. I had money, I had fame, I had an Olympic gold medal, I had won every major snowboarding event I had ever dreamed of winning when I was a kid. And I had poured everything I have into snowboarding.

Apart from that, I didn't have a whole lot going on in my life. I didn't really know who I was and what I was doing. Everyone knew me as Kelly Clark—pro snowboarder; Kelly Clark—Olympic gold medalist, and that's who I was. That's who I was to other people and that's who I was to myself. I was thinking: "If this is what life is, if I've accomplished it all, if this is everything: I don't want to do it anymore."

GOD STILL LOVES YOU

I went to a snowboarding event and from the outside perspective my life was picture-perfect and together. I was doing well in the contest and I qualified for finals that afternoon. But at the bottom of the pipe this girl had fallen on both runs and was crying. Her friend was trying to make her laugh and said: *"Hey, it's all right, God still loves you."* There was just something about that comment that I couldn't shake. It stirred something up in me.

So I ran back to my hotel room and I thought: "There has got to be a Bible in the hotel room… there are always Bibles in hotel rooms, right? As I started looking at the Bible, I realised that I didn't know where to look or where to start. I found out that the girl who made the comment was staying in my hotel. I knocked on her door and said: *"Hey, my name's Kelly and I think you might be a Christian and I think you need to tell me about God."* And at the same time I got nervous because I had never thought about God before a day in my life. I had never once wondered why we are here, I had never thought about Him, never been to church, nothing.

She started to share with me. She cleared up my misconceptions about what being a Christian was. I had thought it was about going to church, and rules and being good all the time. She told me it was about having a relationship with Jesus. I heard about how much God loved me. How He sent His Son to die for us so that we might live. And that God created me for a purpose and that He had a good plan for my life.

DECISION TIME

I spent the next four months thinking: "OK, God, if you're real, reveal yourself to me." I got to the end of my season and I asked myself a few questions like: "Could I ever wake up another day and not think about God?" And the answer was "no" because I was thinking about Him every day and He was real and in my life. Could I ever run the other way and pretend He didn't exist? That answer was also "no." And so I came to a conclusion and said, "Alright, Jesus, come and live life with me."

A NEW HEART

It says in the Bible: *"Rid yourselves of all the offences you have committed, and get a new heart and a new spirit."* (Ezekiel 18 v 31). It also says: *"I will give you a new heart and put a new spirit in you; I will remove from you your heart of stone and give you a heart of flesh."* (Ezekiel 36 v 26). I felt like God switched on my heart. I never knew it worked. I know that sounds crazy but my heart was so hard, I was so far from allowing myself to be loved by anyone.

God changed all that. I felt like I was alive for the first time. So that's my story. I had everything but nothing at the same time. Through all of that I never found happiness, purpose or love like I have found in Jesus. Through my relationship with God I learned who I was, and was comfortable in who I was. But I'll tell you, I've never had more fun snowboarding, and I've never been more free.

70 ACTS: Paul on tour

Paul's still touring around, telling people about Jesus and helping start up new churches. Next, he reaches Ephesus, a city known worldwide for its huge temple to the goddess Artemis.

Read Acts 19 v 1–10

ENGAGE YOUR BRAIN

▷ *Who haven't these disciples heard of? (v2)*

▷ *Which type of baptism have they had? (v3)*

These guys knew about John the Baptist (Jesus' cousin who was the support act who paved the way for Jesus), but they didn't know much about Jesus Himself.

▷ *What had John told people to do? (v4)*

▷ *What do they do as a visible sign they now believe in Jesus? (v5)*

▷ *What amazing things happen? (v6)*

The Holy Spirit doesn't enable eveyone to speak different languages or prophesy. But He does make a difference to everyone He lives in, just in different ways.

THINK IT THROUGH

▷ *Who does the Holy Spirit live in? (v4–6)*

Sometimes Christians worry they need something extra to really have the Holy Spirit living in them; a special experience, baptism, or service. But if you believe in Jesus as your Lord, then the Spirit lives in you! Christians get baptised as a sign that Jesus has turned their lives around. That's the consistent message of the apostles; look back to Peter's words in Acts 2 v 38.

TAKE IT FURTHER

More surprises on page 121.

71 | Man, not machine |

What does Jesus mean to you?
How would you describe Him in one sentence?
How do you treat Him?

👁 Read Acts 19 v 11–16

ENGAGE YOUR BRAIN

▶ How did God show that Paul was His servant? (v11–12)

▶ Describe what happens in v13–16 in your own words.

▶ What did these guys think saying "the name of Jesus" would do? (v13)

They thought that Jesus was like a machine, to be used as they wanted. If they said:6 *"In the name of Jesus, come out"*, hey presto, the demons would come out. But Jesus isn't a machine; He's someone we need to know and relate to as a person.

THINK IT THROUGH

We may not try to use Jesus to get rid of evil spirits; but we can try to use Him as a machine in other ways, as a mechanism who'll do what we want. We need to treat Jesus as the person He is; speak to Him, hear from Him, relate to Him as a someone, not as a something.

These guys got it wrong; let's see some other guys getting it right.

👁 Read verses 17–22

▶ How did these men show they truly respected Jesus?
v18:
v19:

They completely turned away from the fake things they'd been trusting in, despite the cost.

PRAY ABOUT IT

Talk to Jesus now. If recently you've not been spending much time talking and listening to Jesus, ask Him to forgive you and make sure you get back into the habit.

THE BOTTOM LINE

Treat Jesus as a person to relate to, not a machine to be used.

➡ TAKE IT FURTHER

Grab some more on page 122.

72 ¦ I predict a riot

You may have noticed that when Paul talks about Christianity, it often ends in a riot. We've seen that in Ephesus lots of people had put their trust in Christ — but today the riot kicks off.

👁 Read Acts 19 v 23–27

ENGAGE YOUR BRAIN
▷ *What's Demetrius' job? (v24)*
▷ *What's his problem with what Paul's been saying? (v25–26)*
▷ *What does he think the result of this will be? (v27)*

THINK IT THROUGH
▷ *Why are they opposed to Paul's message?*
▷ *What does this suggest about why people might oppose Christianity today?*

It's not because they think it's not true, but because they see it will change things and perhaps make life tougher for them.

👁 Read verses 28–34
▷ *How do Demetrius' buddies react? (v28)*
▷ *What happens? (v29–34)*

Notice they're not explaining why they think Paul's wrong. They're opposing him not with reasoned argument, but with ranting and aggression. Some of them don't even really know why they're there! (v32)

👁 Read verses 35–41
One guy, the city clerk, doesn't get carried away. He calms the crowd and sends them home before much damage is done.

PRAY ABOUT IT
Ask God to help you keep talking about Jesus even when you face opposition. Ask God to remind you that gospel success provokes gospel opposition. Pray for Christians who live in countries where talking openly about Jesus provokes aggression — that God would give them the courage to keep sharing the gospel.

THE BOTTOM LINE
Gospel success provokes gospel opposition.

➔ TAKE IT FURTHER
Riot and wrong on page 122.

73 | Is Paul the real deal?

You listened to this guy Paul... you put your trust in Jesus... and since then there's been rioting and threats against you. Was it really a good idea to listen to Paul?

👁 Read Acts 20 v 1–5

Paul sails to Macedonia to encourage the Christians there (v2).

👁 Read verses 6–12

▷ *In Troas, how does one guy react to Paul's epic talk? (v9)*

If you've ever nodded off in a Bible talk, you're not the first! At least you didn't die!

▷ *What does Paul do? (v10–11)*

What on earth's going on here?! To get this episode's significance, let's rewind 1,000 years, to the time when Elijah was God's chief messenger.

👁 Read 1 Kings 17 v 17–24

Elijah's staying with a widow. When her son dies, she thinks Elijah's presence has brought only trouble.

▷ *What happens next? (v19-23)*

▷ *What does she realise about Elijah because of what she's seen? (v24)*

The widow needed reassuring that Elijah really was God's messenger, and that it was worth listening to him. God reassured her by acting powerfully through Elijah to bring life to the dead.

THINK IT THROUGH

The Christians of Troas needed reassuring that Paul really was God's messenger, and that it was worth listening to him. God did this in a spectacular way.

Paul's the real deal. And the centre of Paul's message was that through Jesus, God can give life to the dead.

▷ *How do these Christians feel? (v12)*

THE BOTTOM LINE

Paul is God's chosen messenger; we can trust what he says.

➔ TAKE IT FURTHER

More stuff on page 122.

74

Crucial qualities

Most churches have a pastor; some have several. What's the job description for a pastor? Pretty funny, friendly, remembers names? Or is there more to it than that? What would be your top three criteria for a church pastor?

👁 Read Acts 20 v 13–17

Paul's on his way to Jerusalem. He's in a hurry, but stops off at Ephesus to speak to the leaders of the church he set up there.

👁 Read verses 18–21

Quality #1
▷ *What did Paul do as their pastor? (v19)*
▷ *Was this easy for him to do? Why, or why not? (end v19)*

Quality #2
▷ *What did pastor Paul preach, and where did he do it? (v20)*

"Helpful" is an interesting word. Pastor Paul didn't only tell people what they wanted to hear, but what was helpful — what they needed. And he didn't only do it on Sundays.

Quality #3
▷ *What else did Paul spend his time in Ephesus doing? (v21)*

THINK IT THROUGH
Sum up pastor Paul's three crucial qualities in your own words:

1 —

2 —

3 —

PRAY ABOUT IT
It's pretty hard being a pastor. There are testing setbacks; there's lots of work to do; there's rarely much thanks. So pray for the pastor (or pastors) at your church now; and commit to praying every week for them, that they'd be like pastor Paul in what they do.

THE BOTTOM LINE
Pastors serve Jesus; preach helpfully; and share the gospel.

→ TAKE IT FURTHER
No *Take it further* today.

75 | Racing through life

How much do you value your life? Is there anything worth more to you than enjoying a good life?

👁 **Read Acts 20 v 22–24**

ENGAGE YOUR BRAIN

▶ Where's Paul going, and why?

▶ What does Paul know will happen when he gets there? (v23)

Paul's not being over the top here. In the last few cities he's been to, he's been caught up in riots, imprisoned, flogged, arrested and mocked. Paul certainly didn't have an easy life. Here's a question: why didn't he stop? Why go to Jerusalem when he knew what kind of things were facing him there? He's done loads for Jesus — why not retire?

▶ Why won't Paul settle for a comfortable life? (v24)

▶ What two things matter to him more than his life? (v24)

THINK IT THROUGH

▶ Do you think Paul is right to have this view of things?

▶ Why, or why not?

▶ How much do you value your life?

▶ Is serving Jesus worth more to you?

▶ How is Paul's attitude a challenge to you?

PRAY ABOUT IT

None of us find it easy to look at life the way Paul did. We need God's help to have this attitude — why not ask Him for it now, if you can do so and genuinely mean it?

THE BOTTOM LINE

"I consider my life worth nothing to me, if only I may finish the race and complete the task the Lord Jesus has given me."

→ **TAKE IT FURTHER**
Race ahead to page 122.

76 How to be a good shepherd

Sheep are simple animals. Basically, they need two things; grass to eat, and protection from wolves who'll eat them.

Read Acts 20 v 25–28

ENGAGE YOUR BRAIN

Paul calls the members of a church a "flock": so their overseers, or leaders, are "shepherds".

▶ *Why's the church so precious? (end v28)*
▶ *If you're a Christian, how does it make you feel to be described like this?*

Sheep need feeding...

▶ *What had Paul preached and proclaimed to them? (v25–27)*
▶ *What food do Christians need?*

Sheep need protecting...

Read verses 29–31

▶ *What's going to happen to this flock? (v29)*
▶ *What does Paul mean by this? (v30)*
▶ *What should the shepherds, and the sheep, do? (v28, v31)*

GET ON WITH IT

Paul's talking to the leaders of a church; telling them to copy him in feeding the flock with all of God's truth, and protecting the flock by opposing people who want to distort God's truth. Maybe you're a leader of a group at your church (Sunday school, youth group, etc); Paul's talking to you. Are you feeding and protecting?

Maybe you're not a shepherd — but if you're a Christian, you're a sheep! Make it easier for your shepherd to look after you; get to church regularly, be eager to hear all of God's truth (even the difficult bits), and watch out for anyone who tries to change what God says in the Bible.

PRAY ABOUT IT

Pray for your pastor(s) again; that God would show them how to feed and protect their flock.

→ TAKE IT FURTHER

More on Ephesus on page 123.

77 | Keep going!

Paul brought the message about Jesus to Ephesus; he set up the church in Ephesus; he's taught the Bible to the Christians of Ephesus. How on earth will they keep going now that he's leaving? Can they manage without Paul?

👁 Read verses 32–35

ENGAGE YOUR BRAIN

▷ Under whose care does Paul know these Christians are? (v32)

▷ How will God keep caring for them? (v32)

In His undeserved kindness (grace), God will build them up and one day they will live with Him in perfection.

THINK ABOUT IT

▷ Why would this be of great comfort to Paul as he left?

▷ Why would this humble Paul as he left?

▷ Why would this encourage the Ephesian Christians as he left?

▷ Do they need Paul?

▷ What is the one thing that they do need to keep going?

👁 Read verses 36–38

▷ What do Paul and his Christian friends make sure they do before he leaves?

We're not told what they said; but we can guess from v32–35. Surely they thanked God for His grace to them, and asked God that in His grace He'd keep building them up in their faith and get them to their eternal inheritance with Him.

PRAY ABOUT IT

Spend some time praying for God's ongoing grace for yourself. Then pray for His ongoing grace for particular Christian friends of yours.

THE BOTTOM LINE

God's grace keeps His people going.

→ TAKE IT FURTHER

Hard work on page 123.

78 | ISAIAH: City of dreams

Now for more about that future day of the Lord. For God's people, it will be a day for singing like they've never sung before.

👁 Read Isaiah 26 v 1–6

ENGAGE YOUR BRAIN

▶ How are God's true people described? (v2)

▶ What will they be celebrating? (v1)

▶ Why can God's people trust Him? (v4)

The next chunk picks up the idea of waiting for that day.

👁 Read verses 7–19

▶ How should God's people respond to His discipline? (v8–9)

▶ How do others respond to God's goodness and punishment? (v10–11)

▶ What exactly has God done for His people? (v12–15)

Isaiah describes both the pain of living in this world (v10–18) and the hope

for God's coming new world (v7, v12, v15, v19). We live with this tension. We just have to wait, longing for the time we'll live in God's perfect new creation (v8–9).

👁 Read verses 20–21

▶ What are God's people waiting for?

▶ What's the only way to prepare?

In that final day, God's anger won't be directed against His trusting people (since Jesus faced it on their behalf), but against His enemies — everyone that opposes Him. Nothing will escape His attention (v21).

PRAY ABOUT IT

Check out verse 19. Thank God for promising to resurrect everyone who trusts in His resurrected Son. Ask God to give you the patience to wait for His return.

→ TAKE IT FURTHER

Just a little bit more on page 123.

79 | Slaying the sea monster

Time to fight a sea monster. This one's called Leviathan and stands for all the forces of evil that battle against God and His people.

👁 **Read Isaiah 27 v 1–6**

ENGAGE YOUR BRAIN

▶ What will happen to the "sea monster"? (v1)

▶ What will God do for His people ("the vineyard")? (v3)

▶ Yet what unbelievably gracious offer does God make to His enemies? (v5)

▶ And what will be the future for God's people? (v6)

What a reversal! Instead of the vineyard being invaded, God's people will spread through the world (v6). Because of Jesus, even people from enemy nations can turn to God and make peace with Him. And God's people (Christians) will spread the message of Jesus around the world.

▶ How can you be more faithful and spread the message further?

👁 **Read verses 7–13**

▶ What would God do to this disobedient people? (v8)

▶ Why? (v11)

▶ Yet what will God one day do for His faithful followers? (v12–13)

Here, Isaiah is talking about the fruit of God's judgment. But this punishment of His people isn't the last word — it removes sin and purfies His people (v9). When Jesus was punished on the cross, He removed the sin of everyone who trusts in Him. And one day, God will personally gather individuals from across the world to be members of His people in the new Jerusalem.

PRAY ABOUT IT

Only you know exactly what you want to say to God today.

→ **TAKE IT FURTHER**

Before and after on page 123.

80 | Drunken priests

Chapters 13–27 of Isaiah were all about God punishing enemy nations and the coming day of judgment. Chapter 28 starts a new chunk which focuses on God punishing His own people, with hints of an undeserved rescue.

👁 Read Isaiah 28 v 1–13

ENGAGE YOUR BRAIN

▷ *How does Isaiah describe Israel (Ephraim's) leaders? (v7–8)*
▷ *What will happen to Israel? (v2)*
▷ *But what was the surprise ahead? (v5–6)*
▷ *Yet how did people treat Isaiah's message from God? (v9–10)*

Israel's proud, drunken leaders treated God's words like meaningless baby talk, so God would punish them.

👁 Read verses 14–22

▷ *How did God view Israel's alliance with Egypt? (v14–15)*
▷ *What would He do? (v21–22)*
▷ *Yet what's the next hint of a brighter future? (v16)*

👁 Read Isaiah 29 v 1–8

▷ *What would happen to Jerusalem (Ariel)? (v1–3)*
▷ *But then what? (v5–8)*

👁 Read verses 9–16

God's people ignored His word and trusted in Egypt for protection. So God would blind them to His truth.

👁 Read verses 17–24

▷ *Yet what's the big turnaround for God's people? (v18–19)*
▷ *And how would they treat God differently? (v23–24)*

Get the message. God hates sin and will severely punish anyone who rejects His words (and the message of His Son). And yet, even for pathetic sinners like us, there's a chance of a bright future with God. And it's all down to Jesus (hinted at in 28 v 16).

THINK AND PRAY

What characteristics of God do we see in these chapters? Praise God for His fairness in judgment and the undeserved rescue He offers. Think about how you should respond to His judgment and mercy.

➔ TAKE IT FURTHER

A weird tale on page 123.

81 | Trust the Lord

Yesterday Isaiah gave us some general principles of judgment and mercy, but today it's time to name names: JUDAH, why would you trust EGYPT instead of THE LORD, against ASSYRIA???

👁 Read Isaiah 30 v 1–14

ENGAGE YOUR BRAIN

▷ *How did God describe His people? (v1)*

▷ *How had they stubbornly disobeyed the Lord? (v1–2)*

▷ *What was the problem with their plan? (v3–5)*

▷ *How else does God describe His people? (v9)*

▷ *What terrible things did they say? (v10–11)*

▷ *So what would happen? (v12–14)*

👁 Read verses 15–33

▷ *What should Judah have known all along? (v15)*

▷ *What's amazing about v18 given Judah's attitude?*

▷ *What's the great news for those who call to God for help? (v19–21)*

▷ *How is God's day of judgment described? (v25–28)*

▷ *Yet how will God's people react? (v29)*

👁 Read Isaiah 31 v 1–9

▷ *How does Isaiah sum up God's message? (v1)*

▷ *What must the people do? (v6)*

Of course, God's predictions came true. Judah trusted the Egyptians to protect them, but Assyria smashed Egypt and turned on Judah. But King Hezekiah led the people to repent and turn back to God and the Lord rescued them (it's in chapter 37).

THINK AND PRAY

▷ *What do you trust in more than God? Your own abilities? Money? Intelligence? Relationships?*

Turn your answer into an honest prayer to God, using 30 v 15 as your focus.

THE BOTTOM LINE

Trust in the Lord alone.

→ TAKE IT FURTHER

More final day stuff on page 124.

82 | Transformer

Loads to read today — no time for a brilliant intro!

Read Isaiah 32 v 1–8

ENGAGE YOUR BRAIN

- What will this new king be like? (v1)
- What would people finally realise? (v5–8)

Transformation! God's perfect King (Jesus) will bring justice to the sinful world. God's people will be transformed and everyone will see the foolishness of their sin.

Read verses 9–20

- What was the warning to these women and to anyone who was smugly satisfied with their sinful lives? (v9–14)
- Yet what would eventually happen? (v15–20)

Transformation! God's judgment would be terrible but He would pour out His Spirit (v15) to undo the destructive effects of judgment. The Holy Spirit is now doing that transformation job on all believers, shaping us to be more like Jesus.

Read Isaiah 33 v 1–6

- What would happen to vicious Assyria? (v1)
- What did God's people pray? (v2)
- What awesome truths could they hold on to? (v5–6)

Transformation! Destructive Assyria would be destroyed and God's people would finally turn to Him for help.

Read verses 7–24

- What was the reaction to God's talk of punishment? (v14)
- How are believers described? (v15–16)
- How can you work on being more "righteous"?
- What will God's new Jerusalem be like? (v20–24)

Transformation! God's people will be transformed and will live in the perfect city with no sin, illness or suffering. God will be their King.

PRAY ABOUT IT

What has blown you away today and how will you respond?

→ TAKE IT FURTHER

More Spirit stuff on page 124.

83 | The future's bright

The Lord is King. A King as incredibly holy as the God of Israel won't let people challenge His reign for ever. Those who persist in rebelling against Him will feel the full power of His anger.

👁 Read Isaiah 34 v 1–10

▶ *What was the terrifying news? (v2–4)*

What a grim picture. Nothing but ongoing, eternal punishment. No rescue, no possibility for change. Ever. Those who reject God will be given what they've chosen — hell.

👁 Read Isaiah 35 v 1–10

▶ *How will the picture change for those who trust in God? (v1–2)*

▶ *Why can God's persecuted people stand strong? (v3–4)*

▶ *Who is God's highway to heaven for? (v8–9)*

▶ *Who's it not for?*

▶ *What will life be like for God's people? (v10)*

In a sin-filled world, where believers are opposed and hated, there's a real hope. God's terrible judgment on sin will actually mean rescue for His people. God's perfect King (Jesus) will rule forever. On the last day, some will go away to eternal punishment and some to eternal life. Don't say you were never told. Trust God's promises, not your own perceptions. Right?

PRAY ABOUT IT

The future's bright for Christians. Take some time to sing your praise to God — thinking about the songs of everlasting joy that we'll sing in God's perfect new world.

→ TAKE IT FURTHER

Owls and hyenas on page 124.

84 | Scare tactics

Isaiah has been telling the people of Judah all about God's judgment, on both His own people and the nations who rejected Him. But now we cut to some real action: Assyria v Judah.

👁 Read Isaiah 36 v 1–10

ENGAGE YOUR BRAIN

▷ What'd Assyria already done? (v1)

▷ How did King Senna taunt Hezekiah? (v4, v7)

▷ How did he twist the truth? (v7, v10)

Jerusalem was in big trouble. Assyria had already captured all the other fortified cities of Judah. And now King Senna was trying to scare King Hez into giving up. Hezekiah hadn't really trashed God's altars (v7) — it was because they were used to worship idols. And Sennacherib wasn't serving God (v10) — he was in it for his own power and glory.

👁 Read verses 11–22

▷ How did the Assyrians try to scare the people of Judah? (v11–12)

▷ What did they say about King Hez? (v13–15)

▷ How did Senna try to win over the people? (v16–17)

▷ What huge error was he making? (v18–20)

The big question for Hezekiah and God's people was: who do you trust? They'd been relying on the Egyptians — not God — to rescue them. Assyria was conquering everyone. Could God really help the people of Jerusalem? We'll find out tomorrow.

THINK IT OVER

It's a good question to ask yourself: who do you trust? Who do you rely on? Yourself? Family? Friends? Money? Something else? Talk to God about where you put your trust and ask Him to help you rely on Him.

THE BOTTOM LINE

Who do you trust?

➡ TAKE IT FURTHER

Nothing to be scared of on page 124.

85 | God vs Assryria

Assyrian King Sennacherib has been taunting and terrifying the people of Judah. Will King Hezekiah trust God and turn to Him for rescue, or will he chicken out?

👁 Read Isaiah 37 v1–13

ENGAGE YOUR BRAIN

▷ *What did King Hez finally do right?*

▷ *How did God encourage Hez? (v6–7)*

▷ *But what was the message from the Assyrians? (v9–13)*

👁 Read verses 14–20

▷ *What does Hez recognise about Assyria? (v18)*

▷ *How is God more powerful? (v16)*

▷ *And what does King Hez ask God to do? (v20)*

▷ *Why? (end of v20)*

👁 Read verses 21–38

▷ *Why would God punish King Senna? (v23–24, v29)*

▷ *What should Senna and Hez have known about God? (v26)*

▷ *What did God promise the people of Judah? (v30–32)*

▷ *But what happened to Assyria and its king? (v36–38)*

Sennacherib insulted God and boasted of his own achievements, but it was all part of God's plan. God would save His people and restore His honour. The Lord showed the Assyrians exactly who was boss by wiping out thousands of them as well as King Senna. And the news was good for God's people — God would keep His promises and a remnant would survive.

THINK IT OVER

This was King Hez's finest hour — he finally realised that God was King and nothing was impossible or hopeless. Think what it will take for you to submit to God's rule like this. Will you recognise He's in charge now, or learn the hard way?

THE BOTTOM LINE

God is in control and always keeps His promises.

→ TAKE IT FURTHER

Get a prayer boost on page 124.

86 | Future shocks

God rescued King Hezekiah and Jerusalem from superpower Assyria. Today we read about another incredible rescue for King Hez. But how will he respond?

👁 Read Isaiah 38 v 1–8

ENGAGE YOUR BRAIN

▶ What was the bad news? (v1)
▶ How did Hez react? (v2–3)
▶ What was God's brilliant promise? (v4–6)

👁 Read verses 9–22

▶ What do the four images in v12–14 say about how Hez felt?
▶ But what brought an amazing turnaround? (v15–16)
▶ How did he view his suffering? (v17)

God rescued Hezekiah from death. Guess what, He does the same for us! On the cross, Jesus defeated sin and death for ever. Everyone who trusts in Him will live for ever with God.

👁 Read Isaiah 39 v 1–8

▶ How did Hez respond to this Babylonian's flattery? (v2)
▶ Where had he put his trust?
▶ How did God's punishment fit the crime? (v5–7)

▶ What positive did Hez take from this? (v8)

Hezekiah (like God's people in the Old Testament) refused to trust God's promises and so sparked God's punishment. A devastating glimpse of defeat, captivity and exile to come (v6–7). So... would exile in Babylon be the end? Was there hope of recovery for God's people? Had God cancelled His promises of a new Jerusalem?

No. Yes. No. Throughout Isaiah so far, we've heard about God's punishment of His people for turning away from Him. But we've also seen loads of hints of a better future for those who stick with God. The Lord keeps His promises. We've all turned away from God, yet He gives us far more than we deserve. Jesus has made it possible for all believers to live in God's dream city. Take time to thank and praise God right now.

→ TAKE IT FURTHER

There's no *Take it further* today.

87 | Blast from the past

History. Are you bored by looking back into the events of history or do you find it interesting? This psalm writer found that looking into the past helped him with his present pain.

👁 **Read Psalm 77 v 1–9**

ENGAGE YOUR BRAIN

▷ What was this guy's state of mind? (v1–3)
▷ What were his 6 doubts? (v7–9)
  1.
  2.
  3.
  4.
  5.
  6.

This was a painful time, affecting his heart, soul, mind and body. For God to get tired of His people, to stop showing love, to cancel His promises, to stop being merciful, to be full of anger... it's unthinkable. How could He? But that's not really how things were. Time to look to the past...

👁 **Read verses 10–20**

▷ What did this guy decide to do in his time of doubt? (v11–12)
▷ What did he remember about the Lord? (v13–14)
▷ What specific event? (v15–20)

Rather than dwelling on his doubts and worries, he made himself think about what God is like and remember some of the amazing things God had done for His people. Including rescuing the Israelites by parting the Red Sea.

Doubt can both harm and help. Use it to help you. Don't stew on it in self-pity — take your questions to God. And decide to remember the facts of God's rescue. We can look back to Jesus' death and resurrection as the way God has rescued us. Let these events in history remind you of how much God cares for you.

PRAY ABOUT IT

Take your doubts, worries and questions to God right now. And don't forget to thank Him for the amazing way He rescued you.

➡ **TAKE IT FURTHER**

Big questions on page 125.

88 ¦ Remember remember

Time to sprint through a huge psalm. It's a review of God's people from slavery in Egypt to the time of King David, and it's eye-opening stuff.

👁 Quickly read verses 1–16

ENGAGE YOUR BRAIN
- ▶ Why's this psalm important? (v4–8)
- ▶ Why did Ephraim (Israel)'s army not succeed? (v9–11)
- ▶ Why was this so dumb? (v12–16)

True faith will involve personal trust, careful thinking and obedience. But a failure to remember truths about God, coupled with arrogant disobedience, will be disastrous.

👁 Blast through verses 17–39
- ▶ How did God's people treat Him? (v17–20)
- ▶ How did God respond and why? (v21–22)
- ▶ Yet how did He show them undeserved love? (v23–29)
- ▶ And how did they respond? (v32, v34–37)
- ▶ How did God react to their ungratefulness? (v31, v38–39)

👁 Read verses 40–55

- ▶ What should they have done? (v42)
- ▶ How did God care for the Israelites? (v52–55)

👁 Read verses 56–72
- ▶ Why else did they deserve God's punishment? (v58)
- ▶ How did He punish them? (v60–62)
- ▶ But then what did He do? (v68–72)

Then the psalm ends. Just like that. God's great rescue act gets forgotten (for Israel it was the exodus; for us it's Jesus death and resurrection). And it results in us rejecting God. And Him writing us off.

GET ON WITH IT
- ▶ How can you make sure you remember the cross daily?
- ▶ How will you make sure you talk about it more?

➔ TAKE IT FURTHER
Remember to turn to page 125.

89 | Trouble in the rubble

This psalm was written just after the armies of Babylon had trashed Jerusalem, inflicting God's punishment on His people (it's in 2 Kings 24 – 25). The writer, Asaph, is outraged and full of complaints to God.

👁 Read Psalm 79 v 1–8

▷ *What shocking thing has God let happen? (v1)*

▷ *How did other nations view God's people? (v4)*

▷ *What did Asaph want to know? (v5)*

▷ *What did he ask God to do? (v6)*

▷ *Why?*

▷ *What did he appeal to God for? (v8)*

👁 Read verses 9–13

▷ *Why does he think God will rescue His people and punish their enemies? (v9)*

▷ *And how should God's people respond to His rescue? (v13)*

The situation in Jerusalem was desperate. Asaph urged God to act because...

- His people were in a mess (v1–2)
- they were being mocked (v4, v9)
- He punishes those who reject Him (v6)
- He forgives those who turn to Him (v8)
- He deserves honour (v10)

THINK IT OVER

Even in the struggle of his faith, Asaph managed to look ahead to a time of praising God and telling everyone about Him.

▷ *What has this psalm taught you about God?*

▷ *How will it affect the way you talk to Him?*

PRAY ABOUT IT

Turn to God right now with your struggles, worries, sadness, hopes and praise.

→ TAKE IT FURTHER

Find the sheep on page 125.

READING Psalm 80

90 A vine day

"God, all-powerful Judge, the one who's committed Himself to His people, you Shepherd of your people, restore us" is the way psalms might say it. "God, we really need your help. Now" is how we might put it.

👁 Read Psalm 80 v 1–7

ENGAGE YOUR BRAIN

▶ What do God's people desperately want? (v1–3)

▶ What had they been through? (v4–6)

Joseph, Ephraim, Benjamin and Manasseh = Israel, God's people. The psalm might be looking back on God's judgment on Israel — when He sent Assyria to invade and trash it. They were desperate for God to rescue them and lead them again.

👁 Read verses 8–19

The vine here is God's people — the Israelites. He rescued them from slavery in Egypt and gave them a new land, driving out their enemies (v8). But they turned away from God, so He punished them (v12).

▶ What did they plead for? (v14)

▶ Who would rescue God's people? (v17)

▶ What would be the result? (v18–19)

This psalm's a plea for God to change His people's hearts — to restore them to a right relationship with Him. In Psalm 80, God's people are His "flock", "vine" and "son". The New Testament says Jesus is the Shepherd, true Vine and God's Son. Jesus is now the focus, and God's people are those who trust Him.

PRAY ABOUT IT

▶ What has this psalm taught you to recognise about God?

▶ How might it change the way you pray?

→ TAKE IT FURTHER

A little bit more on page 125.

91 Sing for joy

Praise God. Now. That's an order. Sing up! It's weird being ordered to praise God, but it shouldn't be. God's people have every reason to praise Him, says Psalm 81.

👁 Read Psalm 81 v 1–5

▷ *How should God's people feel about all He's done for them? (v1)*

God acted in judgment on Egypt to free His people (v5). Christians today are to look back to the cross — God achieving our rescue as Christ suffered God's judgment, for us.

▷ *Do people notice your joy about this great truth?*

👁 Read verses 6–10

▷ *What had God done for the Israelites? (v6–7)*

▷ *What did He expect from them? (v9)*

▷ *What do you need to stop "worshipping"?*

👁 Read verses 11–16

▷ *But what happened? (v11–12)*

▷ *Yet what was God's amazing offer? (v13–14)*

▷ *What does the future hold for God's enemies? (v15)*

▷ *And for those who return to Him? (v16)*

The Israelites rejected almighty God, who had rescued them, defeated their powerful enemies and given them so much. Sickening. People who choose to live for themselves are doing exactly the same thing. And the punishment is for God to give them what they choose (v12) — life without Him.

God wanted more than singers: He wanted a people who'd listen to His word and live for Him as their gracious, generous King. Do you live like that?

PRAY ABOUT IT

Time to sing God's praises and commit your life to living His way.

➡ TAKE IT FURTHER

No *Take it further.* Bye!

TAKE IT FURTHER

If you want a little more at the end of each day's study, this is where you come. The TAKE IT FURTHER sections give you something extra. They look at some of the issues covered in the day's study, pose deeper questions, and point you to the big picture of the whole Bible.

1 SAMUEL
The search for a king

1 – FAMILY FORTUNES
Read verses 10–13 again

▶ How does Hannah's prayer compare with the way you talk to God?

▶ What can you learn from Hannah's example?

▶ What will you talk to God about that you've never shared with Him?

We can be completely honest with God. We can tell Him what's on our minds, what's upsetting us. God wants us to pour our hearts out to Him. He cares. He listens.

2 – BYE BYE BABY
Read 1 Samuel 2 v 1–10 and then compare it with Mary's song in Luke 1 v 46–55

▶ How are the two songs similar?

▶ How does v10 in Hannah's song point us forward to Jesus?

The right response to God — in the Old and New Testaments — is faith: an ongoing trust in God. Hannah showed that... how will you?

3 – STEALING FROM GOD
Read verses 12–16 again

The fat should have been given to God — it was the best part. But these guys put themselves before God. And if anyone stood up to them, they were threatened with violence.

▶ What do you keep doing that offends God?

▶ What will you do about it?

▶ Will you say sorry to Him and ask for His help?

4 – PUNISHMENT AND PROMISE
To read more about Zadok, God's faithful priest, check out:
2 Samuel 15 v 24–37
1 Kings 2 v 26–35.

5 – WAKE-UP CALL
Read verses 19–20 again

The stage was set: God's got Samuel in place as priest, prophet and judge of Israel. The boy had become a leader. He would be God's man to choose a king for Israel. He was now a national figure, calling God's people back to living under God's rule.

Read verse 21
and then John 1 v 1, 14, 18
▶ *How has God made Himself fully known?*
▶ *So where should our attention be?*

6 – GOD'S BOX

The ark was a special, gold-covered, portable box which usually sat behind a curtain in the worship centre of Israel — the Holy of Holies. It was a sign that God was with His people, ruling them. These guys used it as a lucky charm, thinking that just taking it into battle would give them victory. That's not faith, it's superstition.

But God doesn't work like that — we can't force Him to help us out or fight our battles. Here we see that God would rather suffer shame than allow His people to carry on a false relationship with Him. We need to think what our motives are with God. Just going to meetings or doing our daily Bible reading won't guarantee God being on our side. He demands total devotion to Him.

7 – GOODBYE GOD

Amazingly on their deathbeds, Eli and the wife of Phinehas got the order right in their relationships. God and His glory is far more important than the closest of human relationships.

▶ *How true is that for you?*
▶ *Are God's glory and honour important to you?*
▶ *How is that seen in your life?*
▶ *How do you need to switch your priorities around?*

8 – GOD VS DAGON

List all the references to hands or the actions of hands in today's reading. Whose hands are involved and what do they do or what happens to them?
v2:
v3:
v4:
v6:
v9:
v11:

▶ *What do these references to hands tell us about the real God and false gods?*

Read Isaiah 46 v 3–13
▶ *What do human hands do there?*
▶ *What does the real God do?*

9 – RAIDERS OF THE LOST ARK

The book of Hebrews tells us that we can stand in the very presence of God because of Jesus (Hebrews 10 v 19–22). However, it also tells us that we're in constant danger of drifting away from Him (Hebrews 2 v 1). Fascinatingly, the advice that Hebrews gives people in this situation is the same as the Philistine diviners give; don't harden your hearts (1 Samuel 6 v 6; Hebrews 3 v 1 – 4 v 1).

For us as Christians, this means continuing to put our faith and trust in Jesus (Hebrews 3 v 12–14) and encouraging each other to stick at it.

▶ *How are you going in these two areas?*

10 – JUST DO IT

Read verse 3 again

This is like the pattern in Judges — God's people sinning against Him, then God letting another nation oppress them as punishment, then the Israelites turning back to God and Him rescuing them. Would their trust in God last this time? Don't hold your breath!

11 – PHILISTINES ATTACK... AGAIN

Read verses 13–14 again

These verses sum up the achievements in Sam's lifetime: God's people were in His land, taking possession of it as He'd intended and promised. Great! But how long would it last?

▶ *What does chapter 7 say about...*
 a) God's character?
 b) God's plans and purposes?
▶ *Which of your answers do you need to remember most?*

12 – DARE TO BE DIFFERENT

Read verses 6–9 again

Don't misunderstand what's going on here! God is not against kings. He promised kings to Abraham and Sarah (Gen 17 v 6, v16; see also Deut 17 v 14-20; 1 Sam 2 v 10).

What's wrong with the request is what lies behind it — a desire to be more like the surrounding nations and less dependent on God.

Think about the things you ask God for. What are your motives? Do you ask for them so that God is glorified or so that life is easier for you, or some other selfish reason? When you pray, think about why you're saying what you're saying.

2 THESSALONIANS
Pray time

13 – PRAY TIME

Read verse 5 again

We say: "Why isn't God doing something about injustice?" Paul teaches us: "He is! He's allowing Christians to go through hard times to get them ready for heaven. And He's letting injustice prevail for a time until His final judgment.

▶ *How does this change your attitude to life now — and in the future?*

15 – TALKING TO GOD

Have you made those prayer lists yet? If not, now's the time. If you have, then maybe you could turn them into a prayer diary.
• Find a notebook and use two pages for each day of the week.
• Divide each double-page spread into four sections.
• Label one *"Who to pray for"* and the

next one *"What to pray for them"*.
- The third can be called *"Praise/thank God for..."*
- And the final section is for you to fill in *"Answers to prayer"*.

What to do with it now is pretty obvious, so get going!

16 –MAN OF LAWLESSNESS
Read verses 10–12 again

▶ *How are those who will be deceived by the antichrist described?*

Such people refuse to believe in the truth. Believing the truth about Jesus demands change — seeking to obey Him and letting Him rule your life. That's too much for many people. But the consequences of rejecting the truth are unthinkable. Verse 11 tells us that God will give them exactly what they've chosen. They want to live without God, so that will be their eternal destiny. Frightening.

17 – MAKE A STAND
Read today's verses again

Thank God for His complete control (sovereignty) over His world; for the prospect of Jesus' ultimate victory; and for His action on behalf of everyone who trusts His Son, Jesus. Ask Him to help you stand firm.

18 – PAUL'S PRAYER POINTERS
Read verses 1–2 again

Paul is completely obsessed with the gospel. He can't stop thinking and talking about it. He wants others to hear and

obey it, and wants nothing and no one to prevent that.

▶ *What are your obsessions and ambitions?*
▶ *What do you hope will happen to you in the next five years?*
▶ *What can you learn from Paul's example?*

19 – JOB SLOBS
Read through the whole letter in one go.

▶ *What have you learned about God?*
▶ *What have you found encouraging?*
▶ *What have you learned about the Christian life?*
▶ *What do you need to change?*
▶ *How will you pray differently?*

ISAIAH
City of dreams

20 – COURT IN THE ACT
When Isaiah was around, God's people had split into two kingdoms — Israel in the north and Judah in the south. Isaiah focuses on Judah during the reigns of kings Uzziah, Jotham, Ahaz and Hezekiah. Let's find out what life was like under those kings.

Read 2 Kings 15 v 1–7

▶ *How would you sum up Uzziah/ Azariah's reign?*

Read 2 Kings 15 v 32–38

▶ *What did King Jotham get right?*

What did he get wrong?

Speed read 2 Kings 16 v 1 – 17 v 20
What did King Ahaz do wrong?

Skim read 2 Kings chapters 18–20
*What good things did King Hez do?
How did his story end?*

All of this was going on while Isaiah was God's prophet, calling God's people back to the covenant — God's promise to be with His people and give them a great life when they obeyed Him.

21 – PURE PUNISHMENT
Read verse 27 again
Zion (another name for Jerusalem, God's people) would be redeemed with justice. God would rescue His people in a way that fits His holiness. He won't pretend sin isn't serious and ignore it. He would require the ultimate sacrifice — the death of His Son in our place. Think how Jesus on the cross shows God's justice *and* His love. Then thank God. More about this later...

Read 1 Peter 1 v 3–9
and pray for Christians you know who are in the middle of fiery tests right now.

22 – FUTURISTIC CITY
Read Matthew 5 v 14–16
Christians should be a light to everyone around them.
▶ *What more could your church or youth group do to show that living with God as King is the best way to live?*

24 – LEADERS OR LOSERS?
Read 1 Peter 3 v 1 – 4 v 1
What makes a woman beautiful in God's sight? (v4)
▶ *How do you need to change your thinking about appearance?*
▶ *What will you do about it?*

25 – BRANCHING OUT
This short chapter is full of promise. Literally. It reaffirms the promises made to Abraham, Moses and David. In the New Testament, we read that Jesus came to the world to fulfil these promises. So this chapter helps to explain the meaning of Christmas!

Check out how Jesus fulfilled the promise of...
• a new king — Matthew 2 v 6
• a holy people — Matthew 1 v 21
• God's presence with His people — Matthew 1 v 23

26 – SAD LOVE SONG
Read Matthew 21 v 33–41
Similar story. The owner is still God, the vineyard is Israel, the tenants are the people's religious leaders, the servants are God's prophets and the son is Jesus.
▶ *What was the owner looking for? (v34)*
▶ *But what kept happening?*
▶ *What did the listeners say should happen to the evil tenants?*
▶ *And the vineyard?*
But they didn't realise they'd spoken against themselves, as the story was all

9...

(cut)

Read verses 42–46
God's people, and especially their leaders, had rejected God's prophets over the centuries. And now they'd rejected Jesus, God's own Son. So God turned to those who would accept Jesus as the world's Ruler and would live lives that produced fruit for God. They'd be God's true people.

Read John 15 v 1–8
In the Old Testament, Israel was often referred to as a vineyard or a vine. But it kept failing to live for God and obey Him. God's people only produced bad fruit.
▶ What's amazing about Jesus' claim? (v1, v5)

Unlike Old Testament Israel, Jesus is the *true* vine. So, being one of God's people now is all about being related to Jesus, being part of His family of believers.
▶ What is the Father's work? (v1–2)
▶ What's His aim? (end of verse 2)
▶ And what's our job? (v4–7)
▶ What will it mean to "remain in Jesus"?
▶ What's the promise if we do? (v5, v7)
▶ And the warning if we don't? (v6)

Read Exodus 33 v 18–23
No one could see God and live! No wonder Isaiah was terrified and felt so dirty. And the thing Isaiah felt worst about was his unclean lips — the sinful

stuff he said.
▶ What "unclean" things do you say?
▶ How can you clean up your mouth?

Read Matthew 13 v 10–17
Jesus uses these verses from Isaiah to explain why He teaches in parables. Some people would reject Jesus whatever they saw or heard and the parables confirm their choice. But Jesus' parables also bring understanding to people who accept Jesus, revealing the secrets of His kingdom to them. God chooses who He reveals the truth to.

Read verse 14 again and then Matthew 1 v 22–23
Jesus is the promised King, born of a virgin. God's people would be scattered, taken into exile far away from their homeland. But King Jesus would end this exile, restoring His people and solving the problems of sin and death. Jesus is Immanuel — "God with us" — sent to rescue God's people.

Read 1 Peter 2 v 4–10
Verse 8 quotes Isaiah 8 v 14. The cornerstone is the most important stone in the building.
▶ What is God's verdict on Jesus? (v4, v6–7)

Many people, including some very important ones, condemned Jesus as a blasphemous maverick and sentenced Him to death. Big shock if they were wrong. And then... God raised Him from death.

🔹 *What are the consequences for those who reject Jesus? (v8)*

🔹 *And for those who put their trust in Him? (v6)*

32 – A NEW DAWN
Read verse 2 again
and then Matthew 4 v 12–17
The promise of new light and new hope comes true in Jesus. He's the King who restores God's people, rescuing us from slavery and exile and bringing us back to God. And just as Isaiah predicted, He began His work in Galilee.

1 SAMUEL

34 – TIME OF THE SIGNS
Read 1 Samuel 10 v 10–13 again
The locals were shocked when they saw Saul joining in with the prophets. They were so surprised that *"Is Saul also among the prophets?"* became a catchphrase when something unbelievable happened.

But someone wasn't so surprised. The guy who said *"And who is their father?"* was probably saying: God's the father of these prophets, so God must have made it happen.

The Lord often uses unlikely people to serve Him in amazing ways. And gives them the ability to do it. Yep, that includes you too.

35 – KING OF THE LUGGAGE
Read Deuteronomy 17 v 14–20

🔹 *What had God predicted 400 years earlier? (v14)*

🔹 *What must Israel's king not do? (v16–17)*

🔹 *What should he be careful to do? (v18–19)*

🔹 *Why? (v19–20)*

🔹 *If the king followed God's guidelines, what was the promise? (v20)*

36 – EYE-OPENING STUFF
Read verse 1 again
The Ammonites were descended from Lot (Abraham's nephew). They regularly tried to capture territory from the Israelites in battle (see Judges chapters 3 and 11).

Read verse 2
and then John 15 v 18–25
God's people must expect opposition from people who hate God and His people and the gospel.

🔹 *Why shouldn't this surprise us? (v18–20)*

🔹 *Why is rejecting Jesus' words and works such a serious thing? (v22–24)*

37 – CELEBRATION NATION
Read verse 14 again
Gilgal was an important place for God's people. It was here that Israel, led by Joshua, first worshipped God after He'd brought them across the River Jordan, into the promised land.

Read Joshua 4 v 19–24

▶ *What great rescue would the crossing remind them of? (v23)*

▶ *What would news of the crossing do for others? (v24)*

▶ *And how were God's people to react to it? (end of v24)*

God's people had been bullied slaives in Egypt, and He'd rescued them by parting the Red Sea. They'd then rejected Him ruling them as king, so He sent them into a desert to wander for 40 years. Yet God still was with them, providing for His rebellious people. Here at the Jordan, He'd done the miraculous again. He'd taken them into the land He'd promised them.

And in 1 Samuel, as Saul and the Israelites celebrated victory, Samuel reminded them of God's greatness and compassion.

38 – FAITHFUL GOD
Read verses 6–13 again

This is so typical. The history of God's relationship with His people showed them that God was a good and loving King and it gave them a pattern to follow. However, they rejected God and asked for a human king. Israel sinned horribly. However, God didn't give up on His people and even used their sinful request in His purposes. Even though they are faithless, He remains faithful. Always.

39 – RAIN OF THOUGHT
Read verse 24 again

What has God done for His people? What has He specifically done for you? Why should that make us fear God? Why should that make us serve Him wholeheartedly?

Ask God's forgiveness for past mistakes and for His ability to make a fresh start and make it last.

40 – SAUL SLIPS UP
Read verses 8–14 again

Saul took on a job that wasn't given to Him by God. He went against God's plans.

▶ *How should he have behaved while waiting for Samuel?*

▶ *What sort of king did God want? (v13–14)*

Saul was behind his own downfall. Next issue we'll meet his replacement, and see a bitter rivalry develop...

41 – DARING RAID
Read 14 v 6 again

➤ *What did Jonathan rightly recognise about the battle? (start of verse) And what else did he know about God? (end of verse)*

It wasn't a random war — God's people were carrying out God's judgment on the Philistines, who refused to worship and obey the Lord.

42 – PHILISTINE PHEAR

Read verse 15 again
For more examples of God using nature to help rescue His people, check out
1 Samuel 7 v 10
and Joshua 10 v 7–14

43 – HONEY BUSINESS

Saul's behaviour was pretty weird, let's face it. But only Jonathan says anything about it, suggesting that his father has "made trouble for the country" (v29).

For two other occasions when this phrase was used, check out **Joshua 7 v 19–26 and 1 Kings 18 v 16–18** and notice the consequences. The king disobeying God could only ever bring serious trouble for God's people.

45 – DESTRUCTION INSTRUCTION

Read verses 2–3 again
God's judgment sounds harsh, doesn't it?

But read Exodus 17 v 8–16
and Deuteronomy 25 v 17–19
Remember that God is perfect and perfectly fair. His justice is always right.

46 – ROYAL REJECTION

Read verse 22
Here's how "The Message" puts it:
"Then Samuel said, Do you think all God wants are sacrifices — empty rituals just for show? He wants you to listen to him! Plain listening is the thing, not staging a lavish religious production. Not doing

what God tells you is far worse than fooling around in the occult. Getting self-important around God is far worse than making deals with your dead ancestors. Because you said No to God's command, he says No to your kingship.

Samuel wasn't saying that sacrifices to God were wrong. He was saying that rituals and formal worship are no substitute for an obedient life.

Read 1 John 2 v 1–6
- ▷ *What makes the truth of v1 such great news?*
- ▷ *How is Jesus the solution to our sin problem? (v2)*
- ▷ *What's a big sign that we truly know Jesus? (v3–4)*
- ▷ *What happens to those who obey Him? (v5)*
- ▷ *How did Jesus "walk"?*
- ▷ *So what's that mean we should do?*

47 – THAT'S TORN IT

Read Hebrews 5 v 7–9
- ▷ *Who was the perfect, obedient king?*
- ▷ *What was He able to do for us? (v9)*

Read Philippians 2 v 5–11
- ▷ *How did Jesus obey His Father?*
- ▷ *How did God respond to this obedience? (v9)*
- ▷ *How should we respond to King Jesus? (v10–11)*

ACTS
Paul on tour

48 – FOLLOW THE DIVERSION
Re-read Acts 16 v 1–3
- *Who does Paul take with him on his journey?*
- *What does he do before they leave? (v3)*

Look back to 15 v 1–2
- *Why is what Paul does to Timothy strange?*
- *What does Acts 16 v 3 say is the reason Paul did this?*

Paul was always absolutely adamant that people did not have to be circumcised to be saved (see Galatians 5 v 2). Has he forgotten that in Acts 16? No — he's circumcising Timothy *"because of the Jews"*. If Timothy was circumcised, the Jews would be more likely to listen to him as he told them about Jesus. So, Paul is clear that we need to do nothing except trust in Jesus to be saved; but that we should do anything legitimate to make it easier for people to listen to our message about Jesus.

49 – MY JOB, GOD'S JOB
We've seen one sign of Lydia's faith in Jesus was that she looked out for the interests of other Christians. Some years later, Paul wrote to the church in Philippi (Lydia's church), reminding them that this should be their attitude to each other.

Have a read of **Philippians 2 v 1–11**, and think about:
- *How is Paul telling Christians to treat each other?*
- *Who is the greatest example of living like this, and why?*
- *Which of these things could you start doing, or do more of?*

50 – POINTS OF VIEW
Re-read verses 19–21
- *Why did the slave girl's owners want Paul and Silas impriisoned? (v19)*
- *So, what was their motivation for opposing Jesus and His people?*

When Jesus gets involved in people's lives, or the lives of those around them, things change. And often people don't like that — so they fight against the gospel message, not because they know it isn't true, but because they don't like its effects.

51 – BE A BEREAN
Because of what happened in 17 v 5–9, and again in v13–15, we might think that Paul's visit to Thessalonica was a failure; and that's what a lot of people from Thessalonica were saying! So Paul wrote to them.

Read 1 Thessalonians 2 v 1–6
- *Did Paul think his visit was a failure? (v1)*
- *What had they been able to do which prevented it from being a failure? (v2)*
- *Whose approval was Paul looking for*

in Thessalonica? (v3)

This is really encouraging for us today. "Success" is sharing the gospel message with someone, however they respond to it, because it's God we want to please, not the people around us. God's pleased when we tell people about His Son, and then it's up to Him how He uses our efforts.

52 – IDOL CAPITAL

Notice that Paul wanted all kinds of people to hear about the resurrection so that they'd recognise Jesus as the one true God. He spoke to religious people (in the synagogue, v17); he spoke to everyday people (in the market-place, v17); he spoke to academic people (in the Areopagus, v19–20). Today, Paul would talk about the resurrection in the church, in the pub, and in the university; and so we should be looking for opportunities in those places too.

▶ *Where will you look for chances to talk about Jesus?*

53 – KNOWING AND NEEDING

▶ *How did Paul know about the altar to the unknown God? (v23)*

▶ *What else had Paul researched about Athens? (v28)*

Paul worked hard to understand what made the people he was talking to tick. By doing that, he was able to point out to them why they needed to hear the gospel message. He began with where they were — worshipping an unknown God — and

then challenged them to listen to the truth about the God who can be known. This is a great lesson for us. If we want people to listen to us about Jesus, we need to understand what makes them tick, so that we can show them why the gospel message is good news for them.

54 – A DAY IN GOD'S DIARY
Read verses 32–34

▶ *What responses does Paul's talk produce?*
  1. (v32a)
  2. (v32b)
  3. (v34)

It's easy to become disheartened when we tell people about Jesus and most of the time they don't want to know. Why can't we be more like an amazing evangelist like Paul?! Well… most people who heard Paul sneered at him; some asked him more questions; and just a few believed. So was it worth it? Of course! A few people turned away from idols and started treating Jesus as God — and gained eternal life. Awesome.

55 – ME? A MINISTER?

Corinth was a huge and massively important city. It was also famous for its "sexual freedom". There was a huge temple to a Greek goddess which employed hundreds of women as prostitutes, and sexual immorality was so common it was almost expected. Not an easy place to go and tell people about Jesus and living His way! Take time out to pray for Christians you know who share the message of Jesus in really tough places and situations.

56 – PAUL'S PANIC

We saw in today's section that Paul was afraid; he gives us more details about how he felt in **1 Corinthians 2 v 1-5**. Read it.

▶ How was he feeling as he talked to them? (v3)
▶ How impressive did he sound? (v1)
▶ But what did he firmly decide he would talk about? (v2)
▶ How's this an encouragement for us?

57 –APEING APOLLOS
Read verses 18–22

▶ When the people in Ephesus asked him to stay longer, how did Paul respond? (v21)
▶ So, did Paul make plans for the future?
▶ But what did he always remember about his plans? (v21)

Humility accepts that God's in charge; pride pretends that we are. It's a point made by another of Jesus' first followers, James, in **James 4 v 13–17**.

ISAIAH

58 – CITY OF DREAMS
Read Isaiah 9 v 8–12 again
People can be so arrogant. They think they can overcome anything, even God's judgment. But that's just not true. God's

punishment is final and devastating.

Read verses 18–21
God's punishment is to take away His love and forgiveness from people. Without God stepping in, wickedness burns like an unstoppable fire. People destroy each other. People reject God and want to rule their own lives, so He gives them what they want — life without Him. And it's horrific.

59 – AXE OF JUSTICE
God had a holy purpose to fulfil (rightly punishing His rebellious people). Assyria's purpose was not so holy — they were crushing nations to show their power. God used Assyria in His plans, but still held Assyria responsible for their godless actions and motives.

Check out Acts 2 v 23, 36–38
▶ How was Jesus the ultimate example of God using something terrible to achieve His perfect plans?
▶ How do we see God in control here?
▶ How should we respond?

60 – BRANCHING OUT
Read verses 10–12 again
The raised banner is the gospel of Jesus. As we spread the word about Jesus, people from every nation are gathered from all corners of the world into God's kingdom!
Pray for people you know from all different parts of whole world. Ask God to help you spread the word to them.

61 – SING YOUR HEARTS OUT
Read 1 Peter 2 v 9–12

▶ *How are Christians described? (v9)*
▶ *So what should they do? (v9)*
▶ *How has God changed their lives? (v10)*
▶ *How can we worship God by the way we live? (v11–12)*
▶ *Who will you talk to about God?*
▶ *How will you live differently as an act of worship?*

62 – BAD BAD BABYLON
Why start with Babylon, rather than nearer enemy Assyria? Two clues...

a) Babylon was already a big power and would soon defeat Assyria and Judah.
b) In the Bible, Babylon isn't just a city. It's also a symbol of everything that defies God (see Genesis 11 v 1–10 and Revelation chapter 18).

One day God will deal with everyone who rebels against Him. In the meantime, every collapse of a proud, immoral regime is a mark of God's judgment and a pointer to the final day that will come.

▶ *How should these truths affect you and your worldview?*

63 – GOD'S ENEMIES DEFEATED
Read Isaiah 15 v 1–9

▶ *How would you describe the general mood in Moab? (v1–4)*
▶ *Amazingly, how did God feel? (v5)*
▶ *What happened to all the riches Moab had stored up?*

People shouldn't act as if God doesn't exist or matter. They should be terrified of Him. If they keep trusting in their own strength and relying on wealth instead of living for the Lord, they will be punished. Horrifically. God doesn't enjoy it (v5), but He won't stand by and watch people sin against Him over and over again.

64 – DREAD ZONE
Read verses 12–14
These verses probably refer first to Assyria but also to all nations/individuals who make war on God.

▶ *Do you ever think you've got a good reason to rage against God?*
▶ *What do you rage about?*
▶ *What does chapter 17 say is the right attitude towards God?*

65 – WALK LIKE AN EGYPTIAN
Read Isaiah 20 v 1–6

▶ *What was God's surprising instruction to Isaiah? (v2)*
▶ *What was this a picture of? (v3–4)*
▶ *What would happen to God's people who'd relied on Cush and Egypt? (v5–6)*
▶ *Who can't we rely on?*
▶ *Who can we rely on?*

66 – VALLEY OF VISION
**Read Isaiah 22 v 12–13 and then
1 Corinthians 15 v 29-32**
If there is no resurrection, then *"eat and drink for tomorrow we die"* is a good policy, because there's nothing after death.

But Christ has been raised and so we too will be raised to eternal life!

What difference should this make to our behaviour?

Read James 1 v 9–11

Should Christians with no money, get down about it? (v9)
What will happen to wealth and to people who rely on money? (v10–11)

Read 2 Corinthians 8 v 9

Thank God for the incredible sacrifice Jesus made. Even though He was richer than we could ever imagine, living with His Father in heaven, He became poor for our sakes. He gave up everything, including His life, for us, so that we can have the unbelievable riches of a relationship with Him.

Read Isaiah 24 v 23 again

The coming judgment of God is one aspect of the coming reign of God. The climax of judgment is that *"the LORD Almighty will reign"*. God defeats His enemies so that He will reign unchallenged. God destroys evil so that He will reign in justice. So, bizarrely, judgment is good news. Judgment is God establishing His reign of peace and justice. Can you see how God's judgment is actually good news?

Read Isaiah 25 v 1–5

Can you use the words of this song to praise God for His coming day? Of course, judgment on its own is not good news at all, because we all deserve to be punished by God for the way we've treated Him. But the good news is that Jesus has taken God's punishment in our place. So those who trust in Jesus can enjoy the blessings of God's perfect reign…

Read Revelation 21 v 1–8

▶ *What will be put in place of the present world order? (v1–6)*
▶ *How would you describe what it will be like? (v3)*
▶ *What will be the fate of God's people?*
▶ *What's the fate of sinners?*
▶ *How often do you think about heaven and eternity?*
▶ *How does this description differ from the way you picture it?*
▶ *How do these verses encourage you to hang in there today?*

ACTS

Read verses 8–10

▶ *What did Paul do in this city famous for superstition and idol worship? (v8)*
🔳 *How did people react to The Way (that's Christianity)? (v9)*
So what did Paul do? (v9)
How effective was Paul's ministry? (v10)

It's estimated that Paul lectured about

Jesus for about five hours a day, six days a week, for two years. That's 3,120 hours arguing about the gospel!

▷ *Could you manage more than 5 minutes talking about Jesus?*

▷ *How can you become more comfortable in talking about Jesus?*

▷ *Who could help you?*

▷ *What do you need to brush up on?*

71 – MAN, NOT MACHINE

Read verses 11–12 again

These verses describe an amazing miracle, even by Acts' standards! Should we expect to see this kind of thing happening in our churches? Should we ask our pastors to bless items of clothing? If we don't see these kinds of things, is there something wrong with our churches or our faith? One word in v11 gives us the answer — "extraordinary". That's what these miracles were: they were out-of-the-ordinary, even for miracles. So while God can work in this way today (He can do anything He likes!), we shouldn't expect Him to; because it's extra-ordinary.

72 – I PREDICT A RIOT

Re-read verses 23–27

▷ *What was the main reason Demetrius hated Paul's message? (v24–26)*

▷ *What did he pretend was his main reason? (v27)*

Demetrius wanted to make money; but he used religion as an excuse for his views. Maybe he'd even convinced himself that he loved Artemis, when in fact all he loved was the money her popularity gave him.

We need to be careful not to do that with Christianity. It's easy to end up loving what Jesus gives us (eternal life, Christian friends, a place in the music band on Sundays, and so on) more than we love Jesus Himself. It's easy to sound as if we care about Jesus, when in fact we care about what we get out of Jesus. Don't do a Demetrius!

73 – IS PAUL THE REAL DEAL?

Read verses 1–2 again

▷ *What's the common theme as Paul speaks to people?*

▷ *Why do you think Paul goes on this tour before heading to Jerusalem?*

▷ *Who can you encourage in the next two days?*

▷ *How will you do it?*

75 – RACING THROUGH LIFE

Read 2 Timothy 4 v 6–8

Paul wrote this to his friend Timothy (who we met in Acts 16 v 1–3) while in prison, facing execution.

▷ *What links Paul's words here to Acts 20 v 22–24?*

▷ *Why is finishing the race worth far more than enjoying a comfortable life? (v8)*

Why not pray, asking God to make your own life one which will allow you to say on your last day: *"I have fought the good fight, I have finished the race, I have kept the faith."*

76 – HOW TO BE A GOOD SHEPHERD
Read Revelation 2 v 1–7

This is Jesus' report on the church in Ephesus, about 50 years after Paul spoke to its elders in Acts 20.

▷ *What are they doing well? (v2, v6)*

▷ *How does this link back to Acts 20?*

▷ *What are they getting wrong? (v4)*

▷ *If they turn back and keep going, what does Jesus promise? (v7)*

This is a useful reminder to us that while we need to make sure we're watching out for people who try to change God's truth, we also need to make sure we're continuing to love Jesus ourselves. We're not to love "getting the Bible right"; we're to love the Lord Jesus, who the Bible tells us about.

77 – KEEP GOING!
Read verses 32–35

▷ *What wasn't Paul in Ephesus to do?*

▷ *What did he work hard to do?*
  v34:
  v35:

This is grace — working hard to give to others instead of looking to receive from others. In His grace, God's Son died on the cross to give others life; in his grace, Paul had laboured so he could help the weak. Understanding God's grace did not just affect the way Paul prayed; it also shaped the way Paul lived, always looking to give rather than to receive. Why not ask God to show you where you can show grace and give rather than receive today?

ISAIAH

78 – CITY OF DREAMS
Read verses 9-11 and 16–18 and then Hebrews 12 v 7–11

Sum up how you tend to respond to difficult circumstances:

a) fight the situation

b) resent it

c) grumble

d) shrug your shoulders

e) get confused and flustered

f) trust God and submit to Him

▷ *What can you do to start getting more f)s?*

79 – SLAYING THE SEA MONSTER
Read Isaiah 5 v 1–7 and then Isaiah 27 v 1–6

Back in chapter 5, Isaiah compared Israel to a vineyard. Now he speaks of another vineyard that will grow "in that day". How do the two compare?

Read Isaiah 27 v 13

Those "perishing in Assyria" and "exiled in Egypt" stand for anyone among the Gentile nations who trusted God. Extend this out and that includes... you! Yes, you. You're part of a world-wide people drawn to God to trust Him. Brilliant.

80 – DRUNKEN PRIESTS
Read Isaiah 28 v 23–29

It's a strange story, but here's how Barry Webb explains it:

"It illustrates God's various ways of working in history. Sometimes He deals

harshly with His people and sometimes He acts with great tenderness towards them. Sometimes he saves them from their enemies; sometimes He gives them over to their enemies. Why do His ways change so much? The parable gives the answer.

A farmer changes his manner of working according to the materials he is working with and the stage he is at. So too the LORD changes His manner of working in history. But His ways are not haphazard; He is working according to a plan. Most of the processes described in the parable suggest pain — ploughing, threshing, grinding — but all contribute to the final good of food production. In a similar way the LORD'S severe dealings with His people are directed towards a good end which He constantly has in view, as we have seen (28 v16, 21)."

81 – TRUST THE LORD
Read Isaiah 31 v 6–7
"That day" means the final day of the Lord, when everyone (willingly or not) will have to admit that God's in charge. Idols will seem ridiculous — why worship anything other than the one true God? Christians now — those who trust God — should always be ready not just to face the next crisis in life, but to stand before God on that final day. Are you?

See how Jesus put it in Luke 21 v 36.

82 – TRANSFORMER
Read Isaiah 32 v 15 again
Since Pentecost (Acts 2), God gives His Spirit to every believer. The transformation He brings about in us, and keeps on doing, will be completed in God's new heaven and earth.

83 – THE FUTURE'S BRIGHT
Read Isaiah 34 v 11–17
What's all this about owls, jackals, hyenas and goats? Well, Edom was an enemy of the Israelites. Here it stands for all God's enemies, who He'd punish. The land would be overrun with brambles and wild animals — it would become desolate. Once-proud nations will be brought low by the Lord. There's no escape for those who reject God.

84 – SCARE TACTICS
The Assyrian commander keeps saying: *"Do not listen to Hezekiah"* (v 14, 15, 16, 18). It must have had some effect on the people listening. We're shaped by what we hear.
▶ *Does what you listen to mostly honour God or dishonour Him?*
▶ *Does what you listen to make you depend on God more or encourage you to depend on other things?*

85 – GOD VS ASSYRIA
Read verses 14 and 21
Those who really trust God needn't panic. Got that? And even when things are our own fault, we can still pray about them. When King Hez prayed, God changed

things. Wow! God listens to His people! So pray!

PSALMS

87 – BLAST FROM THE PAST

So how would you answer the big questions in this psalm?

▶ *Will the Lord reject forever?*
▶ *Will He never show his favor again?*
▶ *Has His unfailing love vanished forever?*
▶ *Has His promise failed for all time?*
▶ *Has God forgotten to be merciful?*
▶ *Has He in anger withheld his compassion?*

What similar questions do your friends ask? Why not grab some other Christians (including some older, wise ones!) and discuss how, using the Bible, you can answer some of the doubts people have about God?

88 – REMEMBER REMEMBER

Read verse 61

The ark contained God's covenant and was a sign of God's presence with His people. So when it was taken away it showed that God had left His people.

Read verses 32–39

▶ *What pattern was getting repeated in Israel's history?*
▶ *What's the psalm teaching us?*
▶ *Do you see yourself behaving like Israel did towards God?*

89 – TROUBLE IN THE RUBBLE

Sheep show up in psalms a few times, revealing to us God's relationship (as the Shepherd) with His people (the sheep).

Check out: Psalm 23
            Psalm 74 v 1
            Psalm 77 v 20
            Psalm 100

90 – A VINE DAY

Read verses 3, 7 and 19 again and then Deuteronomy 31 v 16–18

God hides His face from His people when He is angry with their sin. The face is the gateway to knowing someone. So God hiding His face is the ultimate punishment — not knowing Him or having a relationship with Him.

Read 2 Corinthians 4 v 6

The good news is that we can get to know God through His Son Jesus!

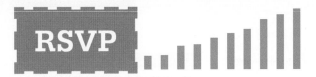

engage wants to hear from YOU!

▶ Share experiences of God at work in your life
▶ Any questions you have about the Bible or the Christian life?
▶ How can we make *engage* better?

Email us — **martin@thegoodbook.co.uk**

(Unlike in previous issues, this email address actually works!)

engage 37 Elm Road, New Malden, Surrey, KT3 3HB, UK

In the next **engage**

Titus The good life
1 Samuel David's rise to fame
Ruth Love story
Isaiah God's rescue plan
Acts The gospel on trial
Plus: Death — what happens next?
Real life stories
Abortion — the lowdown
Saved by grace

Order **engage** now!

Make sure you order the next issue of **engage**. Or even better, grab a one-year subscription to make sure **engage** lands in your hands as soon as it's out.

Call us to order in the UK on `0345 123 0880`
International: `+44 (0) 20 8942 0880`

or visit your friendly neighbourhood website:
UK: www.thegoodbook.co.uk
N America: www.thegoodbook.com
Australia: www.thegoodbook.com.au
New Zealand: www.thegoodbook.co.nz